THE
SCOTCH
WHISKY
BOOK

THE
SCOTCH
WHISKY
BOOK

MARK SKIPWORTH

LOMOND BOOKS

Photographic Acknowledgements

Allied Lyons: 140; Renuka Barnes: 13 bottom; Bartels Rawlings International: 119 top, 131 bottom left, 131 bottom right; Berry Bros. & Rudd Ltd: 33 bottom, 118 top, 118 bottom, 127 left, 143 top, 143 bottom, 145, 152 top; Clydesdale Scotch Whisky Co. Ltd: 104 top, 119 bottom right, 130 top, 138 bottom left, 144 bottom, 151 bottom; Cointreau S.A.: 103 bottom; Findlater Mackie Todd & Co Ltd: 120, 128 right; Gordon & MacPhail Ltd: 109 bottom; J & G Grant: 97 right, 98 top; William Grant & Sons Ltd: back jacket, 2-3, 10-11, 26 bottom, 36, 36-37, 38-39, 40, 42 top, 42 bottom, 43 top, 45 top, 45 bottom, 46 top, 49, 50 bottom, 52, 52-53, 58-59, 60 top, 60 bottom, 62, 63, 64-65, 70, 72-73, 74, 77, 90 top, 98 bottom, 146; John Hannavy Picture Collection: 41 bottom, 47; Highland Distilleries Co. plc: 54-55, 92, 104 bottom right, 115, 128 left; International Distillers & Vintners Ltd: 126 bottom, 131, 139 right; The Invergordon Distillers Holdings Ltd: 91 bottom, 95 right, 105 right, 129 top, 135 right, 139 left, 148 bottom right; John Jameson & Son Ltd: 82; Lonrho plc: 95 left, 110, 116, 141 right; Macallan Distillers Ltd: 109 top; Macdonald & Muir Ltd: 75, 102, 103 top, 122 left, 126 top, 129 bottom, 130 bottom left, 133 bottom, 134 top, 149 top; J & A Mitchell & Co Ltd: 56, 108 right, 113 bottom; Montrose Whisky Co Ltd: 121, 150 bottom right; Stanley P Morrison Ltd: 89 left, 91 centre, 99, 151 top; George Morton Ltd: 119 bottom left; National Gallery of Scotland: 15, 16; Oakfield Ltd: 134 bottom, 149 bottom; Octopus Books Ltd: 84: 85; Old St. Andrews Ltd: 150 top; Photo Source: main cover picture; Robertson & Baxter Ltd: 67 top, 100 bottom, 137 right, 138 top, 148 top; The Seagram Co Ltd: 78, 81 left, 100 top, 101 left, 101 top right, 101 bottom right, 108 left, 135 left, 136, 137 left, 138 bottom right, 144 top, 152 bottom; Scotch Whisky Association: 41 top, 43 bottom, 44, 48, 50 top, 66; Twelve Stone Flagons Ltd: 153 top; United Distillers Group: front cover (inset), title spread, 6, 12, 13 top, 14, 15, 16, 17 top, 18, 19 top, 19 bottom, 20, 21, 22, 23 top, 23 bottom, 24 top, 24 bottom, 25, 26 top, 27, 28, 29, 31, 32, 33 top, 34-35, 51, 55, 56-57, 61, 67 bottom, 68-69, 70-71, 71, 79, 80, 81 right, 89 right, 90 bottom, 91 top, 93, 96, 97 left, 104 bottom left, 105 left, 106, 111, 112, 113 top, 114, 123 top, 123 bottom, 124, 125 left, 125 right, 127 right, 130 bottom right, 131 top, 132, 141 left, 142, 147 left, 147 right, 148 bottom left, 149 centre, 150 bottom left, 153 bottom; Hiram Walker & Sons (Scotland) plc: 83, 122 right; Whitbread & Co plc: 30, 107, 117, 133 top, 133 centre.

Line Artwork by Michael Fisher/The Garden Studio

First published in Great Britain in 1987
by The Hamlyn Publishing Group
part of Reed Consumer Books Limited
Michelin House, 81 Fulham Road, London SW3 6RB

This editon published in 1992 for Lomond Books
by Reed Consumer Books Limited
Michelin House, 81 Fulham Road, London SW3 6RB
and Auckland, Melbourne, Singapore and Toronto

Reprinted 1992, 1993, 1994

Third Impression, 1994

ISBN 0 600 55291 8

Produced by Mandarin Offset
Printed in Hong Kong

CONTENTS

INTRODUCTION

Together with the Royal Family, Scotch whisky is probably the most successful advertisement for the British way of life. It is unquestionably Scotland's greatest gift to good living. For Scotch whisky is an international drink, sold in every corner of the globe, bringing pleasure to millions.

The image of Scotch whisky is of a 'cottage industry' – that of the careful art of the distiller nurtured in the lonely glens and hillsides of the Highlands and Islands. Of course, with single malt whiskies, this is, broadly speaking, the reality. But Scotch whisky is also very much a product of the Scottish Industrial Revolution of the 19th century, and the big grain distillers and blenders who have helped the drink to gain a worldwide reputation, are to be found mainly in or near the major cities of the Lowlands.

That is not to say anyone anywhere can make whisky with the distinctive quality of Scotch. It is unique. Even the Japanese, those masters of mimickry, as well as being enthusiastic whisky drinkers themselves, apparently feel it necessary to import Scotch malt whisky to mix with their own spirit. There must surely be something about the Scottish climate, its water and its peat, not to mention centuries of experience of distilling, that makes it well nigh impossible for those outside Scotland to unlock the secrets of Scotch whisky.

Scotch whisky is a drink of such variety that it is capable of suiting most tastes. As well as telling the story of Scotch, this book will, I hope, be of some practical use. A directory of brands is provided to help both the enthusiast and the occasional tippler to find out more about their favourite drink and to select suitable new ones.

Everyone will have their favourite Scotch whiskies, particularly the malts. I am no exception. For the record, my favourites are: Linkwood, The Macallan, and Springbank, a Campbeltown malt, with an indefinable aroma and the wholesome qualities of a true 'water of life'.

Time-honoured practices and traditional ingredients make the uniqueness of Scotch whisky.

THE SPIRIT OF THE PAST

The story of Scotch whisky is the story of a people who saw themselves as having an inalienable right to Nature's bounty. Distilling was as much a part of their lives as bringing in their harvest, tending their animals on the hills and fishing their salmon. For centuries, they kept their whisky to themselves, distilling mainly for their own use – transforming the barley from their harvest, the peat from their hills and the clear waters from their streams into 'the water of life'.

The origins of the drink are shrouded in mystery. When the mist is not rolling in from the sea, you can make out from the Mull of Kintyre in Scotland the white farmhouses on the green hills of Ireland. In the Dark Ages, the two countries were united by their proximity, sharing a common religion forged by Christian missionaries, and a common language – Gaelic. Small wonder, then, that distilling was common to both countries; in which one the art originated, however, historians have continued to debate.

The word 'whisky' is derived from the Gaelic *uisge beatha*, meaning 'water of life' and its equivalents crop up in other languages including the Latin, *aqua vitae*, and the French, *eau de vie*, which may be familiar. Gradually the word *uisge* became *usky* and eventually 'whisky'.

The oldest reference to whisky dates back to late medieval times. The Scottish Exchequer Rolls for 1494 had an entry of 'eight bolls of malt to Friar John Cor wherewith to make aquavitae' (a boll was an old Scottish measure). By the early 16th century, whisky had apparently become a drink fit for a king – whisky receives generous royal patronage to this day. When King James IV of Scotland was in Inverness, during September 1506, his Treasurer's accounts had entries for the 15th and 17th of the month: 'For aqua vite to the king . . .' and 'For

ane flacat of aqua vite to the king . . . ' One of the earliest references to 'uiskie' occurs in the funeral account of a Highland laird about 1618. Afore ye go, you might say!

The 'spiritual' home of distilling in Scotland must surely be the Highlands. No one who visits that region, loosely defined as the area north of a line drawn between Greenock and Dundee, can fail to be struck by its awesome mountains, silent lochs, empty glens and sea-misty islands. The very absence of people – though it wasn't always so deserted – nurtures a sense of discovery and an air of purity for the visitor that is the Highland's special atmosphere. Above all, is its remoteness. In the 18th century, that remoteness was even more acute: visitors were seldom

The art of distilling is centuries-old, but the basic principles remain the same.

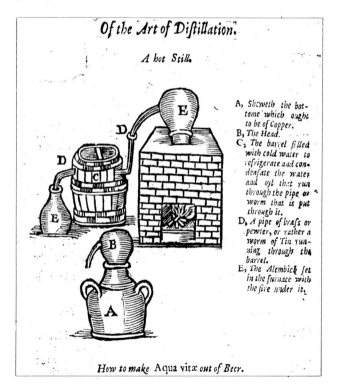

Of the Art of Distillation.

A hot Still.

A, Sheweth the bottome which ought to be of Copper.
B, The Head.
C, The barrel filled with cold water to refrigerate and condensate the water and oyl that run through the pipe or worm that is put through it.
D, A pipe of brass or pewter, or rather a worm of Tin running through the barrel.
E, The Alembick set in the furnace with the fire under it.

How to make Aqua vitæ out of Beer.

tourists – Johnson and Boswell excepted – but rather an adventurer or an English soldier.

Following the Treaty of Union in 1707, which combined the English and Scottish parliaments into that of the United Kingdom, and the failure of the Jacobite cause in 1715, attempts were made to open up the Highlands. You can still see the roads, a network of military routes, built by General Wade for use in controlling the rebellious clans, and places such as Fort Augustus, Fort George and Fort William have their origins in those troubled times. Great feats of engineering though they were, they could only hope to be partially successful in such a mountainous land. Vast areas of the Highlands remained inaccessible to the outsider.

Below: *Nowhere was illicit distilling more difficult to detect than in the Highlands.*

Above: *Illicit stills could be dismantled quickly if the authorities were sighted.*

Whisky production had been hit by taxation under the Scottish parliament. But it was when the British Parliament in 1713 decided to impose a proportion of the English malt tax in Scotland that the great age of illicit stills and smuggling really began. It ensured that illicit whisky was of superior quality to that distilled legally since the legal distillers, to keep the malt tax to a minimum, used a high proportion of raw grain. And it was chiefly the Highlands, with its remote glens and hillsides where whisky could be made undetected, that became the centre for illicit distilling.

The unenviable task of closing down illicit stills fell to the revenue officers – the excisemen or 'gaugers'. Highlanders defied the excisemen by smuggling their illicit whisky into the Lowlands and into England. Thousands of gallons were transported in pigs' bladders and tin panniers hidden in the voluminous dresses of the smugglers' womenfolk.

Among the greatest of the smugglers' wives was Helen Cumming, whose husband John founded Cardhu distillery in Knockando, Morayshire. She was more than a match for the excisemen. There were no inns for many miles, so officers on a visit to Knockando used to lodge at the farm. According to local tradition, as soon as she had prepared their meal and set them down at table, she would steal into the backyard to hoist a red flag over the barn. This was a signal to warn neighbours that the enemy had arrived. The whole area was a nest of illicit distillers.

Tales of outwitting the excisemen have become part of Scottish folklore. In one such tale from Ross-shire, a party of excisemen captured a large cask of whisky which they took to a nearby inn. However, in the room below, smugglers bored up through the ceiling into the cask and drained off all the whisky into a cask of

Distilling was as much a part of the Highlander's life as hunting and herding.

14

Illicit stills were a common feature of life in both Scotland and Ireland.

their own. The excisemen were left without a sample! Stills were discovered in the most unlikely places, from land-locked caves on the west coast, to under the Free Tron Church in Edinburgh's High Street.

Sometimes violence was used against the excisemen: they were bound and gagged, bribed, even killed. But illicit distilling was not considered a serious crime in itself. Magistrates would often impose only a nominal fine on an offender. Government attempts to control illicit distilling only made matters worse – the duty on whisky destined for England reached such a level that it finally damaged the trade of legal Lowland distillers.

The Highlanders continued their illicit distilling undeterred. Their equipment was rudimentary and easy to dismantle, in case they needed to conceal it from the excisemen. Crucial to the distilling process was the 'worm', a copper pipe used to condense the hot vapours from the alcoholic wash into liquid. When the worm had reached the end of its useful life, it was not uncommon for the illicit distiller to report to the exciseman that a still had been discovered, and so claim a reward. With the

money he could then buy a new copper pipe and set up in another glen!

The challenge facing a zealous exciseman was immense. Concerning the Highlands, it was reported in 1798: 'the distillery is in a thousand hands. It is not confined to great towns or to regular manufacturers, but spreads itself over the whole face of the country, and in every island from the Orkneys to Jura. There are many who practise this art who are ignorant of every other, and there are distillers who boast that they make the best possible Whiskey who cannot read or write, and who carry on this manufacture in parts of the country where the use of the plough is unknown, and where the face of an Exciseman was never seen. Under such circumstances, it is impossible to take account of its operations. . . .'

Illicit distilling helped pay the rent of the Highlanders' tenant farms, but it also produced a warming cup for their own consumption to revive their spirits in a cold, damp climate. Whisky was drunk neat or with water, but it was

15

also mixed with water and honey or with milk and honey, or with sugar and butter which was burned until the sugar and butter dissolved. Whisky toddy – whisky, sugar and hot water – was a common drink in 18th-century Scotland, especially in the Lowlands. And the whisky certainly seemed to pack a punch: an English army officer in the Highlands recorded that a group of officers emerged the worse for wear after an heavy whisky session – one was thrown into 'a fit of the gout', another had 'a most dangerous fever' and a third 'lost his skin and hair by the surfeit'!

It was not until 1823 that a new Act of Parliament laid down a cost and taxation basis for whisky which made legal distilling a reasonable proposition for many Highlanders. Around that time, illicit distilling had become so common in Scotland that more than half the spirits actually consumed were supplied by smugglers. In the year of the new Act there were 14,000 official discoveries of illicit stills – surely a fraction of the number that went undetected.

The new Act owed much to Alexander Gordon, fourth Duke of Gordon, speaking in the House of Lords, who helped to initiate change by pledging himself and his fellow landlords to support more moderate laws, and to encourage their tenants to take out licences for their stills. The first to take out a licence was George Smith, a farmer and illicit distiller on Speyside. Shrewder and more farsighted than his neighbours, he realized that the future lay with remaining within the law. With the encouragement of his landlord, the Duke of Gordon, he built a new distillery, The Glenlivet Distillery that today enjoys a worldwide reputation.

The fame of The Glenlivet had already spread far afield before 1823. The fact that it was illicitly distilled made no difference. Even King George IV, who paid a state visit to Scotland in 1822, was presented with some – he reputedly drank nothing else!

Smith's decision to become legal led to great animosity from neighbours who chose to continue smuggling. The very remoteness of his farm became a problem and his regular 35-mile journeys to the coast with pack horses made him vulnerable to attack. He recorded: 'The outlook was an ugly one. I was warned that they meant to burn the new distillery to the ground, and me in the heart of it. I had a pair of hair-trigger pistols and they were never out of my belt for years. I got together two or three stout fellows for servants, armed them with pistols and let it be known everywhere that I would fight for my place to the last shot. Through watching by turns every night for years, we contrived to save the distillery from the fate so freely predicted for it.'

For a decade or more, Smith had to contend with threats but at the same time, he prospered. Output rose steadily, his old pack horse trains were changed for matched teams of fine Clydesdales, which in turn were eventually replaced by steam lorries. A railway line went within seven miles of the distillery by 1863, and a year later the first bottle of The Glenlivet was exported.

Other illicit distillers who followed Smith's example and went legal, also prospered. But others persisted in the old way. It is said that the brewer at Cardhu, who had a croft not far away, made illicit whisky there on his own account at the same time that he was distilling for his employer.

The Duke of Gordon played a key role in the change to legal distilling.

Above: *The men of Cardhu distillery, situated in a remote area on Speyside where early distillers were free from the glare of the Excise.*

Below: *The patent or Coffey still revolutionized the whisky industry, heralding the rise of the blends.*

Though it may not have appeared so at the time, the age of illicit distilling was coming to an end and a new era was beginning. After the new Act distillers had to provide accommodation for the resident exciseman – the 'enemy' had come to stay. From the scandalous heights of 14,000 discoveries of illicit stills in 1823, there were just six in 1874.

The Age of Invention

Distilling in Scotland remained an extension of rural life well into the 19th century. It was the invention of the 'patent still' that revolutionized distilling and laid the foundations of the industry we know today.

Ironically, the patent still that came to be used widely by distillers was invented in 1830 by an exciseman – Aeneas Coffey, a former inspector-general of Excise in Ireland. The Coffey still, as it became known, had some significant advantages over the traditional pot still. It produced whisky more cheaply, quickly and in greater quantities, and the process was continuous (as opposed to in batches). Above

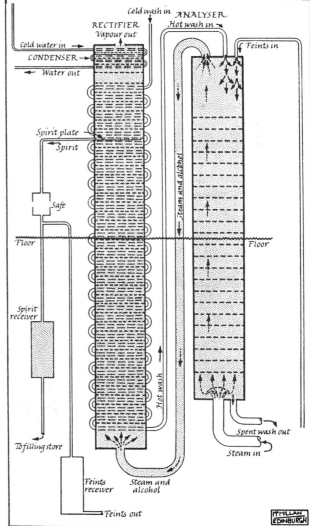

all, it could be installed more or less anywhere –
in the burgeoning towns of the Lowlands, for
example – because, unlike whisky made in a pot
still, the end product did not rely on having the
'right' climate, water and peat to maintain
consistency. This whisky was made from malted
and unmalted barley mashed with other cereals,
and was quite different in character from malt
whisky, which is prepared from malted barley
alone. It came to be known as 'grain whisky'.

It was not long before creative minds were
experimenting with blends of pot still malt and
patent still grain whiskies. There had been some
'blending' before now but it had taken the form
of mixing or 'vatting' different malt whiskies.
From 1860 the Excise permitted the blending of
whiskies from the different distilleries. The
technique of blending – balancing the full-
bodied malts of the Highlands, say, against the
lighter Lowland malts and grains – made possible the emergence of distinctive brands which
were uniform in character from year to year and,
it could be argued, appealed to a wider public
than malt whiskies.

Among the greatest of the early blenders must
surely be William Sanderson of Leith who
founded William Sanderson Ltd., in 1863.

William Sanderson (left) *staged an elaborate tasting where
Vat 69 was born* (below).

A Punch *cartoon of 1848 – the English market had yet to
be conquered by Scotch whisky.*

Sanderson began as a wine and cordial manufac-
turer and, like a medieval alchemist, would
experiment with different mixtures. Appropriately, the blended whisky which was to become
the company's most celebrated brand was born
– so the story goes – of an experiment of the
most elaborate nature. In July 1882, Sanderson
made up nearly 100 different blends of malt and
grain whiskies, placing each one into a separate
container and giving it a number. Expert
blenders and friends were invited along to
choose the best one. Everyone agreed on the
blend in the vat numbered 69 – Vat 69 had
arrived.

By the middle of the 19th century the patent
still distillers of the Lowlands were well established. Their product, along with some malt
whisky, was used in England for making gin
where it was re-distilled and flavoured. Faced
with competition from distillers south of the
border, the Lowland patent still distillers
entered into a trade agreement to protect their
shares of the market. But it was not until the
1870s that it was proposed to form the leading

grain distilling companies into a single company – the Distillers Company Ltd., which was to become synonymous with Scotch whisky.

The growth of a wider market really began with the Franco-Prussian war, which created boom conditions in the iron and coal industry of the Lowlands. So, throughout the 1870s, miners and steelworkers enjoyed high wages and sales of blended whisky soared. But Scotch whisky had to wait until the last decade of the 19th century before it conquered the English palate – and it needed a stroke of luck to do so.

Traditionally, the Englishman's drink was brandy and soda. But by the 1880s the production of cognac had virtually ceased following the ruin of the French vineyards by the deadly *phylloxera* insect. By the 1890s cognac stocks were so low that the English brandy drinker now needed to look for a suitable alternative. The grape was replaced by the grain.

Curiously, rivalry between Scotch whisky and cognac occasionally re-surfaces today. This is particularly so with malt whisky which is often portrayed as an ideal 'after-dinner' drink in preference to cognac. And at a much-vaunted 'blind tasting' recently of selected malts and cognacs, experts were unable to differentiate between them. It's an experiment worth trying. But given Scotch whisky's international standing today, perhaps the cognac enthusiasts should be claiming victory – after all, their cognacs taste like malt whisky!

Of course, despite the difficulties in the cognac industry, Scotch whisky could well have slumbered on as a popular drink north of the border only, and failed to stir the English market, had it not been for the dynamism, ingenuity and boldness of its greatest salesmen. It was the great whisky blenders and distillers – Haig, Dewar, Buchanan, Walker and Mackie (of White Horse fame) – who seized the moment. Of the so-called 'Big Five' salesmen, it was Dewar, Buchanan and Mackie who were probably the most colourful.

The new thirst for Scotch whisky.

A GOOD HEARING FOR MASTER.

(Honoured Guest at big Country-house is invited by affable Butler to walk through the Cellars. After passing bins innumerable of choicest Vintages, they come to a cask marked " Whiskey.")

Guest. "AH! HA! SO YOU'VE BEEN LAYING IN THE FASHIONABLE DRINK, I SEE! THE DOCTORS ARE ALL MAD ABOUT IT."

Affable Butler. "YEZZIR—LESS HACID, THEY SAY, IN GOOD MALT WISKY THAN IN ANY FORM OF ALCO'OL. I'VE TOOK TO IT MYSELF. IN FACT, I MAY SAY I'VE QUITE GIVEN UP CHAMPAGNES, CLARETS, BURGUNDIES, AND 'OCKS!"

The salesmanship of the Dewar brothers (John Alexander, left; *Thomas Robert* below) *bordered on genius.*

John (Alexander) and Thomas Dewar were among the first to recognize the importance of the English market. Their father had been a wine and spirit merchant in Perth and is remembered as being the first to sell bottled brands. John remained in Scotland to run the business while his younger brother was packed off to London to sell their wares. As a young man of 21 he knew no one there, but 'Whisky Tom', as he was later known, made a remarkable success of the venture, and soon he had orders from a great variety of hotels and restaurants in the capital. From the earliest times he understood the need to grab the public's attention for his blended whisky by show-stopping actions. This he did to great effect at a brewers' show at the Agricultural Hall in Islington in 1886. There he rolled up with a piper in full tartan and proceeded to

give the lily-livered Sassenachs a blast of the bagpipes!

In time the company acquired its own distilleries, and Tommy travelled the globe promoting Dewar's whisky. Both brothers came to form a formidable part of an elite group of 'whisky barons': John who remained in Scotland became Baron Forteviot of Dupplin while Tommy, every bit the English country gentleman by this time, was named as Baron Dewar of Homestall, Sussex. You can still see the monument to their fame and fortune in London – Dewar House in the Haymarket, built in 1908.

Like the Dewar brothers, James Buchanan made a fortune from whisky. He was something of a slow-starter, founding his own firm at the age of 35. Born in Canada of Scottish immigrant parents, he went from one job to the next never really finding his true 'metier' until he started selling Scotch whisky, as London agent for a Leith whisky company. Thus was he introduced to the capital's insatiable thirst.

Buchanan soon decided to strike out on his own. Having managed to obtain supplies from a

James Buchanan (left) won orders for his whisky (below) from music halls to the House of Commons.

Sir Peter Mackie of White Horse fame was an eccentric of boundless energy.

Glasgow whisky firm he put it in a black bottle with a white label and began selling it with gusto. He eventually called it 'House of Commons' after winning a contract from the House of Common bar. Buchanan's whisky became popular and could be bought in many of the music halls and bars of London. The name that it eventually came to be known by was 'Black and White' which the public invariably asked for because of the distinctive black bottle and white label.

In 1922 Buchanan became Baron Woolavington of Lavington. Like Tommy Dewar, his 'roots' were now in the south of England. Both men took to horse racing, though Buchanan was probably the more successful of the two. His horses won the St. Leger and the Derby during his lifetime.

Peter Mackie has been described as 'one-third genius, one-third megalomaniac and one-third eccentric'. He had trained at the Lagavulin Distillery on Islay, which had been run in part by his uncle. Mackie was responsible for building up White Horse Distillers Ltd., as it became known after his death. He was the champion of maintaining a high standard for Scotch whisky, and was a great fighter for the cause of maturing whiskies.

'Restless Peter' was a true blue Tory and an outspoken critic of Lloyd George, then Chancellor of the Exchequer, whom he referred to as a 'Welsh country solicitor' for his attacks on the whisky trade. He was a man of broad interests – he was a justice of the peace and a keen sportsman. He was also a frustrated explorer, funding the Mackie Anthropological Expedition to East Africa. One of his most bizarre ventures was the making of B.B.M. flour, which stood for Brain, Bone and Muscle – this, he insisted, every employee at his distilleries should use in their own households! The walls of Mackie's Glasgow office held two notices which summed up the greatness of the man: 'Honesty is the best policy' and 'Take nothing for granted'.

Right: *John Haig who built a distillery at Cameron Bridge*. Below: *Johnnie Walker*.

In 1820, John Walker bought a grocery, wine and spirit business in Kilmarnock. But it was his son Alexander, who joined him in 1856, who was really responsible for laying the foundations of the company's success in the 20th century. He exploited Kilmarnock as a centre for carpets and textiles, spreading the name of the family's whisky through the salesmen who came to the town. And he made use of the merchant venturers' system to get the whisky sold abroad.

Alexander went to England and in 1880 opened an office in London. The timing couldn't have been better for the dearth of French cognac ensured a ready market for Scotch whisky. In those days, Walker's whisky was known simply as Walker's Kilmarnock Whisky. It was not until 1908, nearly 20 years after Alexander's death, that the brand name 'Johnnie Walker' began to be used.

Haig has long been associated with distilling. Unlike the other companies that go to make the Big Five, it was not so much the creation of one or two enterprising individuals but more the joint endeavour of a family dynasty. Nor did the business grow up overnight, for it developed gradually. The family history, not surprisingly then, is intricate.

The Haigs were a Lowland family who were

Right: *Alexander Walker*.

active in distilling in the 17th century. By the 18th century the five sons of John Haig were all involved in distilling. One of them, Andrew, went into partnership with a member of the Jameson family who went on to become famous in Irish distilling. Another, the eldest son, James, became a leading Lowland distiller who spoke on behalf of other legal Lowland distillers about their problems before the Government of the day.

It was John's youngest son William who forged links with the Fife region that still exist to this day, by building a distillery there. One of William's two sons, John, is perhaps the most

Above: *Haig's success is not the story of one man, but of a dynasty.*

Below: *William Grant's early distillery workers.*

famous of all the Haig distillers. In 1824 he build a distillery at Cameron Bridge and employed travelling salesmen to ride out spreading the Haig name. He was among the first to introduce the patent still process for the production of grain whisky, and like his uncle, he became a spokesman for the Lowland distillers. He was a founder member of the Distillers Company Ltd. in the year before he died.

The blending side of the business remained independent until 1925 when it was acquired by Distillers. Around that time, the company's classic advertising slogan was introduced ('Don't be vague – ask for Haig'). Like many other whisky producers, the 20th century has seen the company build up exports worldwide.

Haig whisky played its part in one of the great whisky stories of this century. It happened during the Second World War when a consignment of whisky, including Haig, was being shipped to the U.S.A. The ship went aground in the Hebrides off the west coast of Scotland. On board were hundreds of thousands of bottles of whisky and a few casks – more than enough to quench the thirst of the islanders! The story has been immortalized in Sir Compton Mackenzie's book *Whisky Galore* which has also been made into a comedy classic film.

The seemingly unstoppable rise of Scotch whisky received a nasty jolt at the turn of the century. In 1898 Pattison's Ltd., one of the

The Industrial Revolution had a big impact on Scotch whisky.

largest blenders and wholesale merchants, went bankrupt. Prior to this, however, the firm had showered huge orders upon distillers, and the whisky trade had reached a state of over-production that seemed ripe for disaster.

The Pattison family were famed for their often lavish displays of personal wealth. They were said to travel everywhere, even between their home in Dundee and their place of business in Leith, by their own private railway train. Their business premises were on a scale so palatial that John Grant, of Glenfiddich fame, used to say on entering them that he always felt the urge to sing 'I dreamt that I dwelt in marble halls'!

When Pattison's suspended payment of their creditors, the crash that followed brought a number of distilling firms to ruin. And the industry was full of unsaleable surplus stocks of whisky. For some of the more resourceful distillers, this disaster proved the spur to start exporting overseas for themselves.

The Pattison family suffered an ignominious end to the affair – the two brothers, Robert and Walter, who controlled the company, were tried for fraud and sentenced to imprisonment.

Despite the Pattison crash, Scotch whisky had made great strides by the end of the 19th century. It had gone from being a parochial drink to one of broad appeal. Improved communications, one of the corner-stones of the Industrial Revolution, had played their part. In the beginning, whisky in small quantities was transported south by individuals, often cattle-herders. With the growth of the railways, trade was boosted further afield. In 1843, the mainline railway from Glasgow to the south, via Kilmarnock, was completed. This new faster method of transportation meant more business visitors to the town, famed for its carpets and textiles. Many of them travelled home with some of Johnnie Walker's Kilmarnock Whisky in their luggage.

Water transport was also exploited. Distilleries were sometimes sited on the banks of canals to facilitate receipt of raw materials and despatch of the finished product. The Islay distilleries were built by the sea with piers extending from the distillery buildings. Later, in the 20th century, a classic sight was the S.S. Pibroch, a Clyde 'puffer', which came to serve the Lagavulin and Caol Ila distilleries on Islay and the Talisker distillery on Skye. The puffer was so called because its long funnel was always puffing something out – someone called it 'a pillar of smoke by day and a pillar of fire by night'! Full of coal and barley, its distinctive puff, puff, puffing could be heard from the shore on still, summer evenings.

One company which owes a lot to sea-farers for its success is Gordon Graham and Company of Aberdeen, the producers of Black Bottle. The company has been in existence in the city since 1879 and at first, was involved almost exclusively in the importation and blending of tea; Black Bottle Scotch whisky was produced for consumption by the partners, their friends and business acquaintances.

The reputation of the brand spread throughout Aberdeen and the north east coast of Scotland where it was enjoyed by members of the local fishing fleets who carried the product further afield. The result of this was that the tea business was overshadowed and eventually disappeared and the partners devoted themselves to Black Bottle.

Overseas markets were reached through the 'merchant venturer' system, whereby goods were entrusted to the captain of the ship who would sell them on commission at the best price he could get. The system was favoured by the Johnnie Walker company and by this relatively simple means, Johnnie Walker became known throughout the world.

The whisky companies also took it upon themselves to promote their own products overseas and their representatives made world tours to establish markets and set up agencies in many countries.

Right: S.S. Pibroch *was a familiar sight between the island distilleries and the mainland.*

Below: *Caledonian Distillery, Edinburgh.*

The 20th Century

What is whisky? This may seem a curious question for the whisky industry to be faced with in the early years of the 20th century. The uncertainty as to what constituted whisky, however, was brought about by the remarkable rise in popularity of the blends. The solution to the problem, though, had momentous bearing on what we recognize today as Scotch whisky.

The question first arose in 1905, when the London Borough of Islington took out test cases against certain publicans who were charged with selling as whisky a spirit 'not of the nature, substance and quality demanded'. Judgement stood ultimately against the publicans. This meant that patent still whisky was not consi-dered true whisky and that blends containing it were adulterated. The decision sent shock waves around the Scotch blended whisky industry. If the decision was allowed to stand, the industry would surely be ruined.

The Distillers Company Ltd., formed by those early patent still distillers, probably had more to lose than most. They approached the Government on behalf of the grain distillers and blenders as a whole, and urged that the controversy be settled. Their request was granted. In 1908 a Royal Commission was set up and the key issue was whether restrictions should be placed on the materials or processes by which whisky could be manufactured. Their findings were conclusive, if somewhat restrained by the language of bureaucracy: 'We are unable to recommend that the use of the word 'whiskey' should be restricted to spirit manufactured by the pot still malt distillers'.

Blenders and grain distillers alike could breathe a sigh of relief, and the finding proved a turning point in Scotch whisky's long history. Although malt whisky was – and still is – a vital

Left: With improved communications, the reputation of Scotch whisky spread. Fishing fleets carried Black Bottle further afield.

Below: A malt distillery at the turn of the century – still part of the rural economy.

ingredient of blended Scotch whisky, single malt and 'vatted' malt whiskies disappeared as easily available drinks. Blended Scotch whisky had come of age. Well, not entirely. The matter of whether whisky should be matured for a compulsory period of time was yet to be resolved.

The First World War hit the Scotch whisky industry hard. Due to the need to conserve grain, distilling had to be restricted and spirits rationed. During the 19th century, it was only custom and practice to mature whisky. But in 1915, as a wartime measure, whisky for consumption in Britain had to be matured for a compulsory period of at least three years. This minimum period has been with us ever since.

Two years later distilling had to be stopped completely. This was a body-blow for many independent firms which had to close. The grain distilleries of the Distillers Company Ltd., were

The 20th century has seen Scotch whisky become a fashionable international drink, sold in every corner of the globe.

able to carry on, though, producing industrial alcohol for the war effort. After the war, many of the weakened independents agreed to amalgamate with Distillers Company Ltd. The inter-war years also saw that company amalgamate with the major blending firms. Master-minded by William Ross, managing director and later chairman of Distillers, Buchanan-Dewar (who had already joined forces), John Walker, White Horse Distillers and later, William Sanderson came into the company. Haig, the fifth member of the Big Five, was one of the founders of Distillers.

It was around this time that the term 'whisky' came into use to describe Scotch. At the time of the Royal Commission in 1909, the term 'whiskey' with an 'e' was used for Scotch. (Irish whiskey still retains the 'e' and American-made whiskey is usually spelt with an 'e'.)

Over the years the duty on Scotch whisky for consumption in Britain kept steadily increasing, making the distillers jittery about the home market. The industry looked more to export sales, and the U.S.A. became by far the biggest

The U.S.A. is the largest export market for Scotch whisky.

CUTTY SARK

SCOTS WHISKY

from Scotland's best Distilleries
Matured for many years in wood

40% vol   e 75 cl

BY APPOINTMENT
TO HER MAJESTY THE QUEEN
WINE & SPIRIT MERCHANTS

BERRY BROS & RUDD LTD
ESTABLISHED IN THE XVII CENTURY
3, St JAMES'S STREET, LONDON

Product of Scotland

UAF 008

THE LEGEND *of* CUTTY SARK

When the tea clipper Cutty Sark was launched on the Clyde in 1869, she was the fastest ship of her day. As an inspiration to her crew, she'd been given the name of the fleet-footed witch made famous by Robert Burns in his poem "Tam O'Shanter".

In this tale of Scots mythology Tam is chased by a young witch dressed in a "cutty sark" (an old Scots phrase meaning a short shirt). The witch was so fast she managed to catch and tear off the tail of Tam's horse just as they fled across a running stream to safety.

The carved figurehead of the clipper ship now in dry dock at Greenwich in London is a beautiful young witch wearing a "cutty sark".

To celebrate a particularly fast passage, her sailors would make a horse's tail of rope and place it in her outstretched hand.

5 010493 000758

UAR 001

33

importer. In the 1920s, demand for whisky was high, despite Prohibition. In fact, Prohibition had its winners and its losers in the Scotch whisky industry.

Prohibition became law in January 1920. A year later, scenting good business, Francis Berry of Berry Bros and Rudd Ltd., an old, established firm in the heart of London's St. James's, visited his firm's agents in the Bahamas. Not wishing to meddle in the internal affairs of the United States by attempting any whisky-running, it seemed prudent to sell to various 'agents' in Nassau without asking too many questions! Chief among the firm's contacts was one Captain William McCoy, a rum-runner, whose name was to become a byword for good whisky – 'the real McCoy'. When Prohibition ended in 1933, Berry Bros' blend Cutty Sark was already well-known and respected in America. The blend remains one of America's best-selling brands of Scotch.

The town of Campbeltown in Argyll suffered a quite different fate. It had a claim to being one of the whisky centres of Scotland, with no less than 32 distilleries. Such was its importance that even to this day the name of Campbeltown is used to describe a style of whisky, though virtually all the distilleries have gone. Its story is one with a moral: never lower standards to meet fleeting demand. For when the crash of 1929 came, no one would buy the whiskies of Campbeltown and many distilleries had to close.

The Second World War brought problems similar to that of the First: distilling was cut back for long periods and rationing of Scotch introduced. However, exports of whisky went on during the war. Afterwards, such exports became of paramount importance to getting Britain back on its feet. Winston Churchill clearly recognized this: 'On no account reduce the barley for whisky. This takes years to mature and is an invaluable export and dollar producer'.

The Scots could no longer keep their *uisge* to themselves. To help earn badly needed foreign currency after the war, the industry restricted releases of Scotch whisky to the home market. This lasted until 1954, but not until the early 1960s did releases reach their pre-war level. ·

Scotch whisky became an important earner of foreign currency after the Second World War.

Coming up to the Present

Scotch whisky is one of Britain's principal export products. Today exports represent over 80 per cent of all Scotch whisky sales. In 1985 export earnings amounted to £994 million. The United States is the largest export market for Scotch, followed by France and then Japan.

As befits an international drink of good reputation and massive sales, Scotch whisky has attracted big business. You need only look at the names behind some of the popular brands to discover this. And many of them are owned by overseas companies – French, American and Canadian, for example. The Canadian giant The Seagram Company, reputedly the largest alcoholic drinks' firm in the world, is today the proud owner of The Glenlivet, probably the most famous malt distillery of them all, and a whole host of other distilleries and well-known brands. But the biggest name in Scotch whisky is surely that of a company which has associations with Ireland and brewing – Guinness.

On the road – Scotch competes not only with other spirits but also overseas whiskies.

On the wagon – Scotch whisky is very much a big business these days.

In 1985 the company acquired Arthur Bell and Sons, but this was just a taste of things to come. In April 1986, Guinness clinched the 'greatest takeover of all time' with its acquisition of the Distillers Company Ltd. Overnight, Guinness laid claim to over a third of the Scotch whisky market in the UK and more than 40 per cent of that market in the rest of the world.

The 1980s has not been easy for Scotch whisky. In addition to the effects of recession, the industry has had its own problems caused by

over-production of mature whisky and too little demand, both at home and abroad. Distilleries have closed and there have been redundancies. In April 1985, the size of the 'whisky lake' was believed to be the equivalent of two years' supply to the UK market alone! The simple solution – to sell off large quantities cheaply – might produce some return and may create a period of greater demand. It is not surprising, perhaps, that cheaper sub-norms (low-alcohol content spirits) and own-label products in supermarkets and elsewhere are increasingly found. Of course, the risk of over-production is one which the distilleries always face. When the convention is to mature the whisky anything between five and fifteen years as a rule, it can be extremely tricky to predict what demand will be all those years later when the time comes to bottle and sell it.

Scotch whisky is in stiff competition with other spirits, particularly 'white' spirits such as gin, vodka and white rum. And in some quarters, overseas markets are being challenged by Japanese-produced whisky. This is all the more galling for Scotch whisky producers who find their brands, along with other exported drinks to Japan, hit by that country's swinging and discriminatory duties.

Although it only represents a small slice of the market, single malt whisky is doing well. The pioneering work was done by Glenfiddich, the world's leading malt whisky. Such is its popularity that many people do not perceive it as a type of whisky – a malt – but simply as a whisky superior to the other brands behind the bar. About 20 years ago an intensive and skilful marketing campaign, which continues today, transformed Glenfiddich into the world's biggest-selling malt. In 1986, Glenfiddich claimed a 44 per cent share of exports of bottled malt whisky, which means that virtually every second bottle of malt sold is Glenfiddich.

For years blenders have recognized the value of malt whisky, giving their blends character. And now, consumers are catching on to malt, too. Yet it is inconceivable to think of Scotch whisky without the blends. Firstly, many blends are very good, with characters all of their own. Secondly, the companies who control the distilleries see blended whisky as their 'bread and butter' and limit the quantity of malt whisky for sale.

Nevertheless, it is an encouraging sign that malt whisky, once a 'forbidden fruit' unless you knew of a specialist outlet to obtain it, is becoming more widely available. The point was recently brought home to me when reading an advertisement from December 1967 for William Cadenhead Ltd., that excellent firm of bonders and bottlers of rare whiskies. The advertisement was selling single malts including Glen Grant, The Glenlivet, Highland Park, Laphroaig, Springbank, The Macallan and Talisker – all of which are today easily available.

Over the next few years, I envisage that it will be the norm to find 30 or 40 different malt whiskies widely retailed. But if retailers are to be persuaded to stock more malts it is up to us, the consumers, to create the demand. We must set aside our brand loyalties and experiment – an Islay one week, a Highland the next and so on. So it is with particular enthusiasm that I refer you to the single malts section of the directory in this book (see page 88).

Malt whisky is becoming more widely available.
Glenfiddich is the world's biggest-selling single malt
Scotch whisky.

THE SPIRIT OF THE PRESENT

The age of illicit whisky has left its mark on the modern-day malt distilleries. Many such distilleries began life producing illicit whisky, sited in remote areas where not only was there a good supply of water and peat, but also safety from the exciseman. The hills, in the shadow of which many of them grew up, provided the 'pure' spring waters as well as ideal lookouts and much-needed cover. Sometimes they were to be found on the old cattle trails to the Lowlands, possibly at fords where the thirsty herdsmen would stop and receive refres-hement, and agree to take the whisky south (for a profit, of course).

If you are lucky enough to visit a malt distillery in such wild and romantic scenery, do not be surprised to find 20th-century technology bristling behind a quaint 19th-century facade. It may seem that malt whisky distilling has been reduced to the push of a button, but according to Stewart McBain of Seagram, speaking of The

The traditional image of the malt distillery with its pagoda-style roofs.

Glenlivet Distillery: 'As a distiller, you are the guardian of a standard, of an age-old process. Of course, we have added the sophistication of modern methods and practices to the distillery, but we never change the basic principles.'

Malt whisky is made from malted barley only, using the pot still process. Years ago, the barley might well have been grown locally since many of the early distillers were also farmers. Today the industry also uses barley from further afield – from England, Europe and beyond. The process by which malt whisky is made can be divided into four main stages – malting, mashing, fermentation and distillation.

Above: *After cleaning, barley steeped in pure, cold water, long enough to soften it thoroughly.*

Below: *Some distilleries still turn the barley by hand during germination.*

Malt Whisky in the Making

Malting The barley is first screened to remove any foreign matter such as stones or metal. It is then soaked for two or three days in tanks of water known as *steeps*. The wet barley is then spread out on a solid floor known as the *malting floor* and allowed to germinate. Germination may take from eight to twelve days depending on the season of the year, the quality of the barley used and so forth. The temperature and rate of germination must be controlled either by the traditional method of turning the barley by

41

hand on the malting floor at regular intervals, or by mechanical methods in modern plants. It is said that if you can write your name on the wall with the ears, the barley is ready for the next stage. During germination a very important development takes place – the barley secretes an enzyme called *diastase* which converts the starch in the barley ready for conversion into sugar.

At the appropriate moment germination must be stopped by drying the *malted barley* or *green malt*, as it is now called, traditionally in a malt kiln. The floor of the kiln on which the green malt is spread is perforated, so allowing the hot air and smoke from a peat furnace beneath to percolate upwards through the grain. The traditional fuel for this process is peat. (Peat can be thought of as an embryonic form of coal, which it will eventually become under intense and prolonged pressure.) In Scotland, it is also used as a household fuel, and no one could fail to notice its smoky, pungent, sweet smell in any peat-fired home.

Broadly speaking, there are two types of peat:

Above: *Green malt – barley which has been allowed to germinate, but still has to be dried.*

Below: *The kiln floor where the malted barley is spread and then dried.*

42

marsh peat made up of decomposed mosses, and forest peat made up of decomposed leaves and branches. It is marsh peat that is normally used to flavour malt whisky. Once the peat is cut – either by hand or by mechanical means – it is dried out and shrinks to the size of easy-to-handle 'bricks'. Essentially, the smoke from the peat imparts to the malt its characteristic 'smoky' flavour which can later be discerned in the whisky. Of course, different malt whiskies have different degrees of smokiness. A typical Islay whisky will be smokier than a typical Highland, say. To achieve the desired degree of *peat-reek*, it is usual for the peat to be used in the early stages of drying, and coke used to fuel the furnace.

Today the process may be automated and instead of germinating on the distillery floor, the grain is contained in large rectangular boxes – Saladin boxes – or in large cylindrical drums – drum maltings. Air at selected temperatures is blown upwards through the germinating grain, which is turned mechanically. Many distilleries now obtain their malt from centralized maltings

Above: *Peat is cut and dried out before it can be used in the malting process.*

Below: *Drying the malt over a fire in which peat is burned imparts a flavour to the end product.*

43

which supply a number of distilleries. Although they may seem a world away from the pagoda-style malt kilns of the old days, the centralized maltings may be capable of providing the specific peat-reek desired by the individual distillery.

Mashing The dried malt is ground in a mill into *grist* which resembles a coarse flour. It is mixed with hot water in a large circular vessel called a *mash tun*. Here the soluble starch is converted into a sugary liquid known as *wort*. This is drawn off from the mash tun and the solids remaining are removed for use as cattle food.

Fermentation The wort is very hot and has to be cooled before passing into large vessels called *washbacks*. These vessels hold anything from 9,000 to 45,000 litres (1,980–9,900 gals) of liquid. It is in the washbacks that the wort is fermented by yeast. A measured amount of yeast is added and the resulting reaction causes the wort to bubble and froth. After about 48 hours fermentation has turned the wort into a weak form of alcohol, similar to beer, which is known as *wash*. It is from this wash that the distiller ultimately produces the spirit which is to become malt whisky. Such are the similarities with the beer-making process that fermentation is known as *brewing* and the distillery man who supervises is called a brewer. If you visit a malt distillery, be prepared for a surprise when you reach the washbacks. The brewer may well invite you to put your head over the vessel and take a sniff – in my own case the shock from the vapours sent me reeling across the floor!

Distillation Malt whisky is distilled twice in stills which resemble huge copper kettles – pot stills. Their general design has changed little over time. Indeed, of all the equipment used in

Right: *The mash tun – a large circular vessel where the dried malt is mixed with hot water.*

Below: *Some distilleries use a malting process which is carried out mechanically.*

Bottom right: *The gleaming copper and distinctive shape of the pot stills at the Glenfiddich distillery.*

Above: *A washback (where fermentation takes place) showing measuring instruments.*

Right: *The anatomy of a malt distillery.*

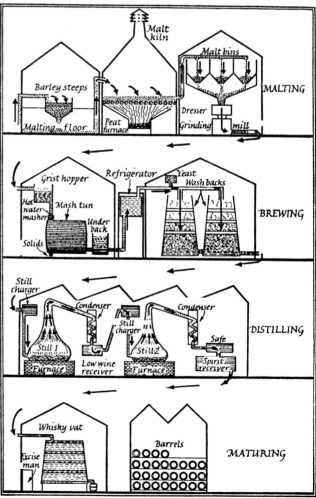

the distilling process, the pot still is the one which distillers are most loathe to tamper with. They are patched up for as long as they can be usefully employed. And when a still has finally to be replaced, the new one will be a carbon-copy of the old, right down to the last dent!

The essence of distillation is straightforward: the spirit is driven off by heat from the fermented liquid as a vapour and is then condensed back to a liquid. In the first distillation, the liquid wash from the fermentation is put into a *wash still* which is heated directly by fire or by steam-heated coils. The wash is heated until the alcohol contained in it vapourizes. The vapour passes up the still and into the cooling plant where it is condensed into a liquid. The cooling plant may take the form of a coiled copper tube or *worm* that is kept continuously cool by running water. This distillate, known as *low wines*, is then passed into the *spirit still* where it is distilled a second time. The spirit still is similar in appearance and construction to the wash still but smaller because the bulk of liquid to be dealt with is less. The liquor remaining in the wash still is known as *pot ale* or *burnt ale*, and is usually processed into animal feed.

The low wines as well as the spirit is subject to government duty and so must be made secure from tampering. As the liquids from the stills condenses it is tested by a *stillman* using hydrometers which, while visible to him, are kept in a locked *spirit safe*. He can thus test the liquid without having to withdraw samples.

As the spirit from the spirit still condenses different portions or fractions of it are separated

Bubbling up a brew in the washbacks – beware if you take a sniff!

and collected, and it is at this point that the stillman really comes into his own. It is only the *middle cut* or *heart of the run* which is of the required strength and quality for malt whisky. Since, however, the middle cut cannot be chosen by tasting or by smell, selection must depend on the unerring eye of the experienced stillman. With the aid of his hydrometer, he knows when the real spirit is running. The first raw runnings, known as *foreshots*, give way to the middle cut on his judgement. The last runnings, known as *feints*, are also decided by the stillman.

Both foreshots and feints are fed back for redistillation with the next low wines. However, it is not unheard of for the stillman to allow some of the feints to be included as part of the middle cut if he considers these add invaluable character to the finished product. Clearly, the great malt distilleries rely heavily on the skill of the stillman for their reputation. One error of judgement could impair their product – an error that might not become wholly apparent until years later during maturation.

I have said that malt whisky is distilled twice. But that is not the full story. There are one or

The spirit safe allows the stillman to test the spirit as it flows from the still. The middle cut, which is of the required strength and quality, cannot be chosen by tasting or by smell – selection depends on the unerring eye of the experienced stillman.

The scale of grain whisky production is much greater than that of malt.

two Scotch malt whiskies which are distilled three times – Auchentoshan and Rosebank, for example, both Lowland malts. And there is a third which could be described as being two and a half times distilled! This is the Campbeltown malt, Springbank, which uses two spirit stills instead of one. One is used for the low wines and the second for redistilling the foreshots and feints.

Grain Whisky in the Making

Grain whisky is made from malted barley together with unmalted barley and maize, in a continuous operation in a patent or Coffey still. To my knowledge there are only two grain

whiskies which are bottled and sold on their own – all the rest are used for blending purposes.

Distillation takes place in two gigantic columns known as the *analyser* and the *rectifier*. Steam is fed into the base of the analyser and hot wash into the top. As the two meet at the surface of perforated plates in the analyser, the wash boils and a mixture of alcohol vapours and steam rises to the top of the column.

The hot vapours now enter the rectifier at the base and as they rise through its chambers, they partially condense on the sections of a long coil

Above: *The copper coils of the Coffey still – a model of economy.*

Right: *Storage tanks at one of the big grain whisky distilleries in the Lowlands.*

through which wash is flowing. The cold wash is on its way down to eventually find its way into the analyser, and this is heated by the condensing hot vapours – a classic economy device and one which is a hallmark of the process.

The spirit vapour condenses at the top of the rectifier and is run off through a final cooling worm to the spirit safe. The unwanted vapours condense lower down the rectifier to be led away for further redistillation. Because repeated distillation is central to the process, the distillate is said to lack many of the 'secondary constituents' found in malt whisky.

The exact nature of these secondary constituents is not fully understood, but it is believed they include some of the essential oils from the malted barley and other cereals and substances that derive from the peat. The amount of these secondary constituents retained in the spirit depends upon the shape of the still and the way it is operated as well as the strength at which the spirit is drawn off. Because grain whisky is said to contain fewer secondary constituents than malt whisky, it has a milder character and requires less time to mature.

What is particularly striking about grain whisky is the ingredients used. The mash consists of unmalted cereals but a proportion of malted barley is still needed – for a very important reason. The unmalted cereals are cooked under steam pressure for about three and a half hours. During this time the mixture of grain and water is agitated by stirrers inside the cooker. The starch cells in the grain burst and when this liquid is transferred to the mash tun, with the malted barley, the diastase in the latter converts the starch into sugar. Without the malted barley acting as a 'catalyst', there would be no alcoholic wash to distill.

Maturation

Of all the processes involved in making Scotch whisky, maturation is probably the most mysterious. Yet, on the face of it, it appears straightforward. Both malt and grain whisky must be matured after distillation has been completed. The new spirit is poured into casks made of oak, which being permeable, allow air to pass in and some evaporation to take place. By U.K. law, both malt and grain whisky has to be matured for three years, and many other countries have similar provisos varying from

Grain whisky production is a continuous process. Controlling it is highly automated today.

Above: *Roll out the barrel – a full cask emerging from a distillery to be stored and matured.*

Right: *New whisky is filled into oak casks and matured in warehouses for a number of years. Maturation is considered essential for the whisky to mellow and its full character to develop.*

three to five years. In fact, in the case of malt whisky at least, leaving the spirit much longer than this is considered essential for its full character to develop. So what are the critical factors involved in maturation?

Location For whisky to qualify for the name 'Scotch whisky', it must be matured in Scotland for three years. 'In Scotland' is vitally important because the Scottish climate seems to have a profound effect on the finished product. As an experiment, Stewart McBain of Seagram sent casks from one distillation at The Glenlivet Distillery to the United States for maturing. On maturation, the results were quite different to those at the distillery. 'Only casks matured here ended up as The Glenlivet. In America, it began well but in three years, the change was quite clear.'

The climate may well affect the volume and strength of the whisky, too. It is said that a whisky which is matured in the damp, misty islands of Islay or Skye will lose its strength more quickly than its volume. Conversely, a whisky which is matured in the dry atmosphere of Speyside will lose its volume more quickly than its strength.

That whisky is affected by the climate seems

less surprising when you consider the long period of maturation. You only have to visit Islay and breathe the air, to see why some Islay malts have a tang of the sea!

Age From the time the casks are filled with new spirit – which has been reduced by the addition of water – the whisky will gradually lose both strength and volume. But the harsher constituents in the new spirit are also removed and a mellow whisky should be produced.

What is the optimum age for Scotch whisky? This is a subject of great controversy within the industry and among experts. It is agreed that malt whisky takes longer to mature than grain whisky. I am told that the character of grain whisky develops little after four or five years in cask. But malt whisky is often left in the cask for fifteen years or even longer. There are some who say this is too long since malt whisky reaches its peak between eight and twelve years of age.

It may be true that some whiskies lose some-

thing of their character by being allowed to mature for too long. But it cannot be said that there is a precise age when malt whiskies in general are at their best. The fashion for selling malts of the same brand but of different ages proves the point. You can buy some of these at 8, 10, 12, 15 and 18 years old. And 1987 sees the promotion of 21-year-old and even older malt whisky on a big scale. All of these whiskies have distinctive characteristics of their own, under-pinned by the general character of the brand –

they are all variations on a theme of quality. It may be that some of these whiskies are better for lunchtime or pre-dinner drinking than after-dinner, or vice-versa.

The view that a whisky of great age is inferior to a youngster of eight or twelve years old, was finally put to rest when I was able to try a 'sherry' The Glenlivet of adult years. It was an experience I will never forget. Quite delicious!

The casks The colour of the new spirit is *clear*. During maturation, it is from the wood of the casks that the whisky is given its colour. And the cask can also impart some flavour and softness. Casks are usually stencilled with the name of the distillery, the year and each one is given a cask number. The number of litres is stencilled on each end after filling. The average size of cask used is a *hogshead* – approximately 250 litres (55 gals). *Butts* are also used, which are twice the size of a hogshead – 500 litres (110 gals) – and *barrels*, which are approximately 180 litres (40 gals).

Left: *The Scottish climate leaves its mark on the finished product. Nowhere is this more apparent than Islay.*

Below: *A cooper sets to work assembling a cask.*

55

Deciding on the type of cask is of key importance to distillers. Traditionally whisky was matured in former sherry casks brought from Jerez in Spain. But these became increasingly difficult to buy, so some malts are matured in wine-treated casks or in new casks. American bourbon casks are also used. Under American law, they can only be used once as bourbon casks, so they are broken down and shipped to Scotland where they are reassembled.

The Macallan, a fine Highland malt, prides itself on using sherry casks only to mature its whisky. The company's directors journey annually to Jerez where they buy oak casks into which they pour sherries of their choice, then keep them for two years in Spain before having them shipped over to be filled with whisky. Is it the sherry casks, I wonder, that gives The Macallan its distinctive oloroso glow?

A good example of one of the new 21-year-old whiskies coming onto the market.

Inside a cooperage at the turn of the century.

But not every distillery wants its malt whisky to have a sherry touch. There are some who see the straw-colour and 'whisky' flavour of their product just as Nature intended. It seems to me that the colour of whisky will play a bigger part in setting the style of brands over the next few years – the 'lights' for daytime drinking, the 'darks' strictly for after dinner. But more about this later.

One of the glories of Scotch malt whisky is that it varies so much from one distillery to the next. But the reasons for this remain unclear. It is said that the water used plays a decisive part. Adjoining distilleries which draw their water from different sources are known to produce whiskies that are markedly different in flavour.

56

Such is the importance of the water source that it determines the siting of a distillery which must be near a good source of supply. Water is needed in order to steep the barley, mash the dried malt and to use for cooling in the distilling process itself. The water flow must be constant, free from the vagaries of the seasons. And it must be free from any impurities that might impair the finished product. That is not to say that it should be 'pure' to the extent that it contains no minerals or peatiness. Some distilleries actually use different sources of water for different operations – a well or burn for the steeping, mashing and so forth, and a sizeable river for cooling.

'There are so many factors that affect the final taste and bouquet,' says Stewart McBain. 'You start to create the character at the malting stage and it continues right through fermentation, distillation and maturation. My experience suggests that the fermentation stage is very important in its effect on the quantity and quality of a malt whisky's character. But so is the long period of maturation and the quality of the cask.'

But he adds: 'We really know so little of what actually happens in the cask as the whisky matures. Fresh young spirit gathers character, smoothness, and subtlety from wood, from the Highland air, from the natural elements – barley, peat, water. But why the results are so different in different places, we do not know.'

A Note on Bottled Scotch Whisky Unlike some wines, Scotch whisky does not improve in the bottle. There is no change in a whisky once

Top: *The busy cooperage at Glenfiddich.*

Above: *Grain whisky uses millions of gallons of water.*

Right: *Filling the casks.*

Preceding pages: *Whether a river or a spring, water is central to whisky production.*

it has been bottled and securely sealed. As oxygen in the air cannot get to the whisky, there is no further maturing. It is also a common misconception that whisky in a bottle loses its strength with age. It does not.

If there is an age on the label, this will mean that the whisky has been matured for this amount of time in the cask – not in the bottle!

Blending and Bottling

Blended whisky is by far the biggest-selling Scotch whisky, and is sold all over the world. Somewhat quaintly, the Scotch Whisky Association which represents the principal whisky companies, echoes the words of former times when speaking about blended whisky's success: 'The reason for this is that pot still malt whisky is inclined to be too strongly flavoured for everyday drinking, especially by people in sedentary occupations and warm climates.' This is doubtful to say the least. There are many single malt whiskies, especially the Lowland ones and some Highland ones, which are light

and drinkable all through the day. Nevertheless, it is the blends that have brought Scotch whisky an international reputation, so perhaps one should not be too critical.

Blending is the skill of combining mature whiskies from several different distilleries, malt as well as grain. (The combining of malt with malt – or grain with grain – is known as *vatting*.) A blend will consist of anything from 15 to 50 different whiskies, combined in a formula that is the secret of the blending company. The proportion of malt and grain will differ from one blender to another. No company is prepared to reveal the proportions of the different individual whiskies used.

The object of blending is to produce a whisky of a definite and recognizable character. But it also to achieve consistency – the blend should never vary from the standard that customers have come to expect. To be able to do this can take many years of experience. Each whisky for blending has a character of its own and some may prove incompatible with others. The malts and grains in a blend must be chosen to complement and even enhance their respective flavours.

The normal practice is for the blender to buy the whisky as soon as it is distilled. It is then kept under bond in warehouses at the distillery to mature until the blender requires it. The big blenders buy mature whisky only when they happen to find themselves short of a particular type or make. It is then they may need the

Left: *The beginnings of a blend. A blend will consist of anything from 15 to 50 whiskies, mixed in a blending vat.*

Below: *The blender usually buys whiskies for his blend when they are distilled. When the time comes, he will want to check that they have matured properly before allowing them to be mixed together.*

services of a broker who speculates by buying up whisky for this very eventuality.

The character of the blend is also determined by factors such as the ages of the individual whiskies and the manner in which they combine. The blender must decide when the different whiskies are ready to be used in his blend. They are brought from the warehouse where they have been maturing, to the blending establishment, where they are mixed together in a blending vat. They are usually returned to cask and left to 'marry' for a period of months, before bottling. However, some companies prefer to vat their malts and grains separately and only bring the two together before bottling.

Throughout the blending process it is the blender's nose which is the final judge. In the blending room he smells or 'noses' each whisky from a tulip-shaped glass: he has to get behind the initial whiff of alcohol and try to assess its flavour – how round, smooth, mellow it is. It never ceases to amaze me that a blender will nose between 20 or 30 whiskies in one session. I find that after three or four nosings, my sense of smell begins to desert me and I get a nasal-numbing sensation which takes some minutes to wear off! Perhaps the experienced blender is inured to it.

Among the great blenders was John K. Brown of White Horse. He worked for the company for more than 50 years as a blender. He would smell it from the glass, rub some whisky on his hands and then inhale it. The one thing he hardly ever did on these occasions was drink it – great blenders find that unnecessary. John Brown was so attached to White Horse at Port Dundas that he hated to be away from the place. On a Sunday he would propose taking his three small sons to the Botanic Gardens or Kelvingrove Park in Glasgow. But his steps always seemed to lead the family to Port Dundas. He would then 'notice' one or two jobs which needed doing around the place, and in no time at all he had his three sons spending their Sunday afternoon working for White Horse!

Whisky producers depend heavily on the 'flavour memory' of the blender. But if, over the years the blender's memory for taste starts to fade or alter, the actual flavour of the final whisky may change. At the time of writing,

Quality control. The success of Scotch whisky as an international drink has been achieved by the blends.

some interesting work at Strathclyde University in Scotland was being carried out to tackle this problem.

A team at the university were reportedly testing brands of Scotch whisky with the aim of helping to ensure that each brand tastes as it always has done. A volunteer panel of food scientists have been sniffing the whisky during daily 15-minute sessions. They have developed a 'scoring' system to characterize different whisky tastes. It is made up of the combined smell reactions of the panel, enabling any whisky flavour – in principle, at least – to be permanently recorded.

Scent and taste are regarded as overlapping senses, and the researchers have compiled a

The blender smells or 'noses' the different whiskies. Notice the tulip-shaped glasses he uses to assess flavour.

vocabulary of 24 words to describe the taste. Some of the descriptions sound very elaborate – Langs Supreme, for example, is described as 'cream and apple pie, vanillary smooth, almost creamy with a slightly fruity background'. Descriptions range from grainy, malty and nutty to mouldy, soapy, meaty and fishy. In their terms, some whiskies 'taste fruity (like nail varnish), or grassy (like putting your head inside a dustbin full of grass), or even catty (the smell of tom cats)'.

Other groups have attempted to draw up vocabularies which would standardize descriptions of whisky, both blends and malts. This is particularly welcome for us consumers who would benefit from the descriptions in being able to make a more reasoned choice when it comes to buying. I have tried to come up with a selection of tasting adjectives to describe the whiskies in the directory that follows. The terms are simple and self-explanatory – I hope. A list of these is given in the section 'Be your own taste expert' (page 76).

The blend is reduced to the strength required by the addition of water. At this stage a quantity of caramel colouring may be added to bring it to the colour required. The companies maintain that this is necessary to standardize the colour in their quest for consistency. In fact, caramel is added not just to the blends, but also to some malts. The companies argue that if they did not do this, consumers would be alarmed to find their favourite drink one colour one week and a different colour the next. But surely the problem could be overcome by consumer education using advertising as the tool? It seems a great shame that a drink which requires so much skill to produce should be tainted by the addition of colouring.

Some malt whiskies promote the fact that

Below: *Bottling processes have developed a lot since these times. However, crude though they seem today, they were effective in meeting demand.*

they are free from caramel colouring. And one blend, in particular, is renowned for not using caramel – Berry Bros and Rudd Ltd's Cutty Sark. When asked why Cutty Sark was so pale, Hugh Rudd made the celebrated reply: 'Why are other whiskies so dark?'

Blends and single malts are filtered before bottling to remove any sediment. But some companies use a special form of filtering to enable the whisky to retain its brightness at very low temperatures. If whisky is reduced to a low temperature or stored in very cold conditions, it may become hazy. This haze will disappear when the whisky is brought back to a normal temperature. However, it has been found that when whisky is chilled to temperatures below freezing point, the haze becomes a deposit which can be filtered off. The whisky will there-after retain its brightness at low temperatures.

The concern with this method is that if you take the temperature down too far, the haze you end up removing constitutes part of the substance of the whisky – you lose the whisky's character. I must confess that chill-filtering makes me uneasy. Again, the problem is easily solved by consumer education – all that is necessary is a notice on the bottle informing people that the whisky may develop a haze in cold conditions, and that it will disappear when the whisky regains a normal temperature. In fact, some brands now have these notices on the bottle.

The glass bottles are filled with whisky by automatic machines; the bottles are then sealed and labelled. The law requires that when the age is declared on a label for blended whisky, it must refer to the youngest whisky in the blend. So, if a blend is described as being eight years old, the youngest whisky in that blend must have been matured for at least eight years.

This seems an unnecessary burden on *de luxe* blends which contain a higher proportion of older whiskies than *standard* blends. And no doubt it makes them more expensive than they need be. An 18-year old de luxe blend, for example, must have grain whiskies in the blend which have matured for at least that amount of time, even though it is unlikely they will have improved much after about four or five years. A blend should apply only to malt whiskies used.

The whisky is filled by automatic machines into glass bottles which are sealed by one of several methods and labelled.

68

The Excise

Traditionally the exciseman monitored many of the processes involved in making Scotch whisky. Indeed, so vital was it thought that he should always be available that after 1823 distillers had to provide accommodation for the resident exciseman.

But the 1980s has witnessed a radical change in the way the Excise operates. The distilleries themselves are now responsible for keeping their own records and providing their own security against pilfering. The role of the Excise is more as auditors, though spot-checks on distilleries are made.

Symbolic of the distilleries' new responsibilities is the demise of Crown Locks. These locks, good and solid, were to be found at the spirit

The once ubiquitous exciseman.

A typical Islay distillery, sited in the south-east of the island.

safe and the warehouses where the whisky is matured. The distillers now provide their own locks, and of course they have made use of the available Crown Locks. (There has been some trade in Crown Locks as collectors' items.)

That distillers can be relied upon today to monitor themselves is a far cry from the days of illicit whisky. It's enough to make a smuggler turn in his grave!

Single Malt Whisky

Scotch whisky is a drink of great variety. This is particularly apparent with single malt whisky, which is the product of one particular distillery. No two malts are alike. Yet they can be defined according to the region of Scotland where they are produced, each of which has a recognized style. Few people, I think, would confuse a typical Islay malt with a typical Highland one.

There are four main areas which give their names to malt whiskies:

- Highland malts, made north of a line drawn from Greenock on the west to Dundee on the east.
- Lowland malts, made south of that line.
- Islay malts from the island of Islay.
- Campbeltown malts from the town of Campbeltown in Kintyre.

The designation 'Highland' and 'Lowland' in Scotch whisky terms generally follows the geographical division of Scotland with the Highland Boundary fault being the separating feature. But the Highland region also includes a number of islands, including Jura, Mull, Skye and the Orkneys. The vast majority of malt distilleries – some four-fifths of them – are to be found in the Highland region. The biggest concentration of malt distilleries is to be found on Speyside in the Highland region. This area straddles the counties of Morayshire and Banffshire. In contrast with much of the Highlands, Speyside is a broad fertile valley, the River Spey flowing through green fields, gentle wooded slopes and small towns. Around four out of ten malt distilleries are located there.

Of all the islands, Islay possesses the largest number of distilleries with eight. The island's terrain varies from fertile grassland to wild peat moors – whisky and dairy farming have been its principal economic supports for centuries. One of the features of the Islay distilleries is that they

Right: *Grain distilleries like this one here are to be found mainly in the Lowlands.*

Below: *Malt whisky – the finished product.*

are sited beside the sea, with piers designed for the easy off-loading of barley and prompt despatching of the whisky.

The malt distilleries of the Lowlands are few in number and widely scattered. A distillery is sited as far south as Wigtown in Galloway, but others are nearer the major cities of Glasgow and Edinburgh. Campbeltown, once one of the great whisky centres of Scotland, is today a ghost of its former self. But its name is still associated with a style of whisky harking back to better days.

Each group has its own style, ranging from

the lighter malts to the heavier ones. In that order, you would start with the Lowland malts, through to the Highland ones and thence to the Campbeltowns, ending up with the Islays. The contrast between an Islay malt and a Highland malt has been described in extravagant but illuminating terms: the Islay malt is concentrated on the back of the tongue while the Highland malt seems to be split into two parts, one forward in the mouth and one at the rear!

Of course, there are exceptions to these groupings at every turn. Bunnahabhain, an Islay malt, is – though pungent – unusually light

for an Islay and you would have difficulty placing it. More generally, the Highland malts from the islands are quite different from those on Speyside. Highland Park from the Orkneys, for example, is more akin to an Islay than a Speyside.

It is better therefore to keep an open mind about what you expect a particular malt to taste like. The regional styles should only be used as a guide and should not be relied upon – otherwise your first gulp of a newly-discovered malt could come as a shock!

The Malt Whisky Trail

Speyside boasts the only malt whisky trail in the world. A visitor to the region can spend a day stopping off at several malt distilleries where conducted tours are laid on and a few samples are consumed. The 'trail' is approximately 70 miles long and takes in six distilleries, each visit lasting about one hour. The distilleries are: Glenfiddich, The Glenlivet, Glenfarclas, Glen Grant, Strathisla and Tamdhu. They are all open during the summer months.

The distilleries on the trail have their special attractions. Some still use their own malting floors Glanfiddich is one of the few malt distil-

Above: Glenfiddich attracts visitors from all over the world.

Right: Employees of the Glenmorangie distillery emulate photographs from the 1920s.

leries to bottle its own product. In the Glenfarclas reception centre you can see a confiscated illicit still, on loan from the Customs and Excise. It is not in working order since small holes, by regualtion, have been bored through its base!

Malt Whisky Checklist

The single malt whiskies in the directory that follows cover the the Highland, Lowland, Islay and Campbeltown areas. They comprise (with locations where appropriate):

Highland

Aberlour, Aberlour
Aultmore, Keith
Balblair, Edderton
Balvenie, Dufftown
Benriach, Elgin
Benromach, Forres
Blair Athol, Pitlochry
Caperdonich, Rothes
Cardhu, Knockando
Clynelish, Brora
Craigellacghie, Craigellachie
Dallas Dhu, Forres
Dalmore, Alness
Dalwhinnie, Dalwhinnie
Deanston Malt, Doune
Dufftown, Dufftown
Glen Albyn, –
Glenburgie, Forres
Glendullan, Dufftown
Glen Elgin, Elgin
Glenesk, Montrose
Glenfarclas, Ballindalloch
Glenfarclas 105, Balindalloch
Glenfiddich, Dufftown
Glen Garioch, Oldmeldrum
Glenglassaugh, Portsoy

Glengoyne, Dumgoyne
Glen Grant, Rothes
The Glenlivet, Ballindalloch
Glen Mhor, –
Glenmorangie, Tain
Glen Moray, Elgin
The Glenturret, Crieff
Glenugie, Peterhead
Glenury-Royal, Stonehaven
Glenvale, –
Highland Park, Orkney
Inchgower, Buckie
Isle of Jura, Jura
Knockdhu, Knock
Ledaig, Mull
Linkwood, Elgin
Longmorn, Elgin
The Macallan, Craigellachie
Macduff, Banff
MacPhail's, –
Miltonduff, Elgin
Oban, Oban
Old Fettercairn, Fettercairn
Old Pulteney, Wick
Royal Lochnagar, Craithie
Strathisla, Keith
Talisker, Skye

Tamdhu, Knockando
Tamnavulin-Glenlivet, Tomnavoulin
Tomatin, Tomatin
Tomintoul, Ballindalloch
Tormore, Advie

Lowland

Auchentoshan, Dalmuir
Bladnoch, Wigtown
Kinclaith, –
Rosebank, Camelon

Islay

Ardbeg, Port Ellen
Bowmore, Bowmore
Bruichladdich, Bruichladdich
Bunnahabhain, Port Askaig
Caol Ila, Port Askaig
Lagavulin, Port Ellen
Laphroaig, Port Ellen
Port Ellen, Port Ellen

Campbeltown

Longrow
Sheep Dip
Springbank

75

ENJOYING
SCOTCH WHISKY

There is no correct way to drink Scotch whisky – it is entirely a matter of personal taste. But, in my opinion, there are ways of drinking Scotch whisky which bring out its full flavour.

Scotch whisky is a drink that can be enjoyed neat. But not all brands are at their best taken this way. A splash of water can often unlock the aroma and the flavour, particularly with the malts. Whether you should use water straight from the tap is a matter of some controversy. It is said that tap water can spoil Scotch whisky if the water is highly–chlorinated. And, of course, a great deal of tap water is highly-chlorinated – not just in big towns and cities but also in rural areas.

Connoisseurs maintain that bottled mineral waters should be used instead of tap water. But here again, there are pitfalls. Many mineral waters have pronounced characteristics of their own – witness the number of different brands on the market all with their own particular taste. So if you decide to use mineral water, you will need to be judicious in your choice of brand. And, above all only still water should be used; never use carbonated mineral waters, unless you want an alternative to soda water.

Personally, I am sceptical of the virtues of adding bottled mineral waters. The water often seems rather lifeless if it's been opened and kept for any length of time. Cold, well-aerated tap water seems hard to be beat. Interestingly, Thames Water Authority, the supplier of London's water, carbonated its tap water and pitted it against some sparkling waters in a tasting experiment – the tap water beat many well-known bottled rivals!

Putting ice into Scotch whisky is popular all over the world, as is serving it with a mixer such as soda, lemonade or ginger ale. But it seems a waste to add to a whisky which has a fine bouquet and full flavour of its own.

The discerning drinker may keep a number of whiskies for different occasions. There are those whiskies which lend themselves to daytime drinking while there are others which are best after dinner; some make excellent aperitifs, while others you can drink with a meal. Again, some are ideal party drinks – especially with mixers! – while others are better set aside for a special celebration.

Though there is no rule determining the best shape of a whisky glass, some have advantages over others. I am not an advocate of the tumbler, it is altogether too crude for a drink that is often very delicate. Further, lacking the bowl shape of cognac glasses that intoxicating whisky aroma is easily dispersed. In my opinion, a goblet is superior to a tumbler. It is bowl-shaped to concentrate the smell and it has a foot and a stem which make it easier to pick up and swirl the liquid around, thus bringing out the aroma.

One point here: the bouquet of Scotch whisky cannot be improved by warming it slightly. The effect of such warming would only be to increase the rate of evaporation of the spirit, thus speeding up the release of the aroma. But that is not to say that whisky cannot be enjoyed hot. One of the most delicious whisky drinks is the hot toddy. It is an excellent winter warmer and is often given to alleviate the effects of a cold. To make a toddy, you place a spoonful of sugar in a warm glass and add enough boiling water to dissolve the sugar and hot lemon juice. Add a generous measure of Scotch whisky and stir; pour in more boiling water and top up with whisky, stirring well.

Be Your Own Taste Expert

It is impossible to count just how many brands of Scotch whisky there are. There are about 100 well-known brands in the UK and more are exported (the directory covers many of these brands). With such variety, it's fun to compare one brand with another, and you can do this in your own home.

Compare no more than half a dozen brands at one time – the experts taste many more than this, but it's unlikely that your nose and palate will be able to take the strain! Compare like with like – malts with malts, de luxe blends with de luxe blends, and so forth. If you wish to, make a few notes on each of the brands you try.

It is vital that the tasting is 'blind' – that is to say that you have someone conceal the identities of the brands, by covering up the labels. Should you know what the brands are when you come to taste them, it may affect your appreciation.

Put out two glasses for each brand so that you can try it both neat and with a little water. You will also need a white background to be able to judge colour – a white tablecloth should suffice. 'Palate cleansers' – biscuits or bread – to nibble on between drinks are essential so that you can start each new drink afresh. Don't wear perfume or aftershave because this could mingle with the aromas of the whiskies.

Begin by looking at the colour of the whisky. It is not always an indication of what to expect on the nose and the palate, but remember that whisky companies are trying to create a certain image for their brands, and may use colour to suggest 'lightness' or 'heaviness'. You should then sniff, or to use the experts' term 'nose', all the whiskies. It is possible to differentiate between some of the brands on nosing alone, but those which prove more inscrutable, you should sip neat. It may be that in the end only by

Watch the professionals – and get nosing!

77

sipping them with a little water will you finally be able to form a judgement. When nosing the whiskies, try to get beyond the initial whiff of alcohol. Here lies the art of appreciation.

How are Scotch whiskies described? Below are some popular terms to help you: *full-bodied; medium-bodied; light-bodied; mellow; malty; sweet; delicate; smoky; sherried; peaty; aromatic; lingering taste; refreshing; medicinal; woody; clean taste; smooth; dry; sharp; fiery; tangy.*

The best way to begin tasting is to contrast two very different whiskies, and an ideal combination is to be found in the malts – an Islay such as Laphroaig contrasted with a Highland (Speyside) such as Glenfiddich. And if the tasting bug really takes hold, you can move on to discerning which malt whiskies have been used in a blend – start with White Horse.

The Main Types of Whisky

There are four main types of Scotch whisky:

The standard blend This is a blend of as many as 50 individual malt and grain whiskies. The individual whiskies that go to make the blend have usually been matured for about five years, though there are some which have been matured for eight years and even twelve years. A notable 'youngster' is a blend with the charming name of Pig's Nose which is four years old. A standard blend usually costs less than a malt whisky. Some popular brands include Johnnie Walker Red Label, Dewar's White Label and Bell's Extra Special.

The de luxe blend This is a blend which contains a higher proportion of older whiskies than a standard blend, and is usually more expensive. The term 'de luxe' is a subjective judgement, all the same. There is no requirement that a blend should be of a certain age before it can call itself 'de luxe'. So what to one company may qualify as a 'de luxe' blend may not to another. Some popular brands include Chivas Regal, Johnnie Walker Black Label and Old Parr 500.

The single malt This is the product of a single distillery. Most distilleries produce Scotch whisky primarily for blending purposes, but many retain some of their production for sale as single whiskies. A single malt can range from about five years upwards in age – the older the more expensive, usually. In general, a single malt costs more than a standard blend. Some popular brands include Glenfiddich, The Glenlivet and Laphroaig.

The vatted malt This is a combination of different malts. Strictly speaking, it can also mean a combination of different ages of the same malt. The vatted malt was the forerunner of the blend. Today it may take the form of a combination of different malts from the same region, such as Speyside in the Highlands. It is a comparatively rare breed, but some established brands include The Strathconon, Mar Lodge and Pride of Strathspey.

Left and Right: *Two celebrated de luxe blends – big sellers throughout the world.*

Reading the Label

By law, the strength and the liquid measure of the contents must be stated on the label of a bottle of Scotch whisky sold in the U.K. It must also give the name and address of the bottler.

Strength Spirit of 'proof' strength was the standard used to measure strength until the 1980s. Years ago, spirit of this strength was proved when whisky and gunpowder were mixed and ignited. If the gunpowder flashed, then there was enough whisky in the mixture to allow ignition. Such whisky was held to have been proved. If the spirit was weaker than this proof strength, ignition did not happen.

In the 1740s, the Customs and Excise and London distillers began to use Clark's hydrometer – an instrument designed to measure spirit strength. Later, a more accurate version by Bartholomew Sikes was adopted. This was in use in Britain for over 160 years until it was replaced in 1980. In common with other EEC countries, Britain adopted a system of measurement recommended by the International Organisation of Legal Metrology. This system

Labels are a mine of information – those for the same brand may vary at home and abroad.

measures alcoholic strength as a percentage of alcohol by volume at a temperature of 20 degrees celsius.

Most whisky sold in the U.K. is 40 per cent volume of alcohol, but there are a fair number, often single malts, which are sold at 43 per cent volume. For export, a strength of 43 per cent volume is common, though a surprising number are sold at 40 per cent volume. That the U.K. strength is slightly less than for export goes back to the days of wartime rationing. Because grain was in short supply, distillers had to reduce the strength for the home market, and that strength was never revised.

Below are some U.S. proof strengths and their British and European equivalents:

American	British and European
100 degrees proof	50 per cent alcohol volume.
86 degrees proof	43 per cent alcohol volume.
80 degrees proof	40 per cent alcohol volume.

To my knowledge, the strongest Scotch whiskies on the market are all malts: Glenfarclas 105, a single Highland malt, and Highland Fusilier 105, a vatted malt, both of which are 60 per cent

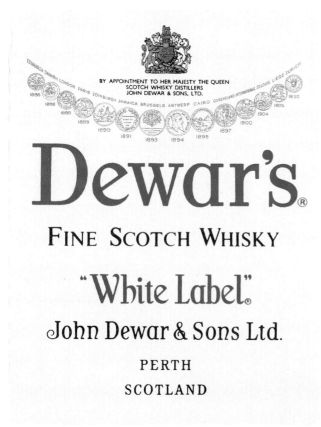

80

volume. But the strongest by a whisker is MacPhail's Gold 106, a single Highland malt, at 60.5 per cent volume.

Contents Such is the variety of liquid volume contents of the bottles used for Scotch whisky that it is virtually impossible to generalize about them. For example, there are more than 600 combinations of different bottle sizes and labels for White Horse covering all the places in the world where it is sold! The contents can be as little as 5 cl. for a miniature going right up to a tregnum (the equivalent of three 75cl bottles). In the U.K., a standard bottle of Scotch is usually 75 cl., though watch out for 70 cl. bottles – something to consider when you're looking for value for money and making price comparisons.

WHISKY GALORE

Although the word 'Scotch' is synonymous with whisky, Scotland – the home of Scotch – is not the only whisky-producing country. Whisky is produced elsewhere in the British Isles and, indeed, all over the world from Argentina to Zambia.

Irish Whiskey

Like Scotch whisky, Irish whiskey gets its name from the geographical area in which it is produced: Irish whiskey means whiskey distilled and matured in Ireland. Two of the most important differences between Irish and Scotch whiskies concern the number of times the spirit is distilled and the ingredients used. Irish whiskey distillers tend to favour three distillations rather than two, as is usual for pot still whiskies in Scotland, and in addition the range of cereals used is wider.

Whether, centuries ago, the art of distilling was exported to Scotland from Ireland remains a matter of controversy. However, the Irish can claim the world's first whiskey distillery at Bushmills which was established in 1608. Like Scotland, Ireland had its share of illicit distilling. It is said that even today, illicit spirit or *potheen* can be had in the west of Ireland. Illicit or not, Queen Elizabeth I of England was said to be fond of a drop of Irish whiskey, long before Scotch whisky had any sort of reputation south of the border.

Welsh Whisky

Not a serious challenger to Scotch whisky, but worth a mention as a curiosity. To my knowledge, there is only one 'chwisgi' – Swn Y Mor – which is, in fact, a mixture of Scotch whiskies. The producer says it can be called 'Welsh whisky' because it has been significantly altered at its final stages in Wales, when the whisky is filtered through native herbs. At a recent

tasting, Swn Y Mor held its own against several big-selling blends of Scotch. The ideal present for a patriotic Welsh friend or relative?

Bourbon Whiskey

Like Scotch and Irish whiskies, bourbon whiskey has a geographical meaning. United States regulations provide that the term 'bourbon' shall not be used to describe any whiskey or whiskey-based spirit not produced in the U.S.A. The regulations also provide that bourbon whiskey must be produced from a mash of not less than 51 per cent corn (maize).

The American whiskey industry goes back to the 18th century, and was founded by Scottish and Irish immigrants who settled in Kentucky and Pennsylvania. The first bourbon was produced in Bourbon County in the territory of Kentucky towards the end of the 18th century. Today, bourbon is made in several states in America and there are reckoned to be nearly 3,000 brands. Not surprisingly, bourbon has a reputation for great variety, akin to Scotch whisky.

The story of whiskey in America is also the story of America itself, particularly in the 20th century. In 1920, the prohibition era began. The thirst for whiskey led to the law being flouted by ordinary people, fortunes being made from sales of the illegal spirit and police corruption. Illicit distilling was rife. In 1921, nearly 96,000 illicit distilleries and stills were discovered. Four years later, the figure had leapt to around 172,500 and, by 1930, to 282,000. Prohibition also allowed Canadian whisky, easily available across the border, to capture a large slice of the market.

Rye whisky

Produced both in the United States and Canada, the name has no geographical significance. However, Canadian whisky is often referred to simply as 'rye whisky' or 'rye'. In the U.S.A., rye whiskey must be produced from a grain mash of which not less than 51 per cent is rye grain. There is no similar restriction in Canada. Canadian regulations merely state: 'Canadian whisky (Canadian rye whisky, rye whisky) shall be whisky distilled in Canada, and shall possess the aroma, taste and character generally attributed to Canadian whisky.'

The Scots and Irish who settled in Canada no

IMPORTED

BY APPOINTMENT TO THE LATE QUEEN VICTORIA 1898 1901
BY APPOINTMENT TO THE LATE KING EDWARD VII 1901 1910
BY APPOINTMENT TO THE LATE KING GEORGE V 1910 1936
BY APPOINTMENT TO THE LATE KING GEORGE VI 1936 1952

ESTABLISHED 1858
HIRAM WALKER & SONS LIMITED
DISTILLERS OF "CANADIAN CLUB" WHISKY

"Canadian Club"
Canadian Whisky
Distilled and Blended under
Canadian Government Supervision by
Hiram Walker & Sons,
Limited
Walkerville, Ontario, Canada.

THIS WHISKY IS 6 YEARS OLD

EX-67-A

doubt brought their distilling skills with them. In more recent times, the movement from east to west has been reversed. Two major Canadian companies, Seagrams and Hiram Walker, bought a host of brands of Scotch whisky and distilleries in Scotland. In particular, Seagrams, reputedly the largest alcoholic drinks firm in the world, owns such distinguished names as The Glenlivet, Glen Grant and Strathisla. Canada's own whiskies are available worldwide, too.

Japanese Whisky

The Japanese are big whisky drinkers. Though they import a fair amount of Scotch whisky brands, they have a thriving whisky industry of their own. This dates back only as far as 1923 when the country's first whisky distillery was built. The industry has progressed in leaps and bounds since that time. However, like certain other 'whisky-producing' countries, they also rely on the import of bulk malt whiskies from Scotland to add to the home-produced spirits. It is argued that Scotch whisky's reputation as a drink of unique quality suffers as a consequence of this. Though it may make economic sense in the short term to export Scotch whisky in bulk at a time when there is an undesirable surplus of stocks, the crunch must surely come when Japanese whisky sales hit Scotch whisky's traditional markets.

A Versatile Drink

Some Scotch whiskies stand proudly on their own, enhanced, perhaps, with a little water. To add other ingredients to them would be to run the risk of adulteration. However, there are some classic combinations which have endured for years, and it is to these that we now turn.

Whisky Toddy. An excellent winter warmer and often given to alleviate the effects of a cold. To make a toddy, you place a spoonful of sugar in a warm glass and add enough boiling water to dissolve the sugar and hot lemon juice. Add a generous measure of Scotch whisky and stir; pour in more boiling water and top up with more whisky, stirring well.

Atholl Brose. The story of how this drink came about goes back to 1475. It is named after the then Duke of Atholl who captured his great enemy, the Earl of Ross, by filling the well at which Ross was known to drink with this potent liquor. The Earl of Ross drank deeply and was taken. This recipe is based on that given by the 8th Duke of Atholl: put three heaped tablespoons of oatmeal into a bowl and mix with about one pint of water until it is a thick paste. Let it stand for about half an hour, then put it through a fine strainer, pressing down well with a spoon so that the oatmeal is quite dry. Throw away the

meal, and mix the liquid with two tablespoons of runny 'heather' honey, and stir with a *silver* spoon until well blended. Pour into a quart bottle and fill up with whisky. Cork well, and always shake before using.

Whisky Mac. A mixture of Scotch whisky and green-ginger wine. It's really a matter of taste how much of each you use – they may be in equal proportions, or two-thirds whisky and one-third green-ginger wine.

Cold Whisky Punch. A pleasant summer drink. Peel three lemons and squeeze out of the juice, then put them in a large jug with half a pound of sugar. Pour two pints of boiling water over and leave until cold. Strain into a large bowl and add a bottle of Scotch whisky, stirring well. Chill for at least one hour.

Whisky Sour. Add the juice of half a lemon to a double Scotch, plus half a teaspoonful of sugar. Shake with ice and serve with a squirt of soda water. A **Scotch Tom Collins** is more or less the same, except you should leave out the sugar, and pour it into a large glass and fill with soda water.

Flying Scotsman. Shake three glasses of Scotch whisky with two and a half glasses of Italian Vermouth, one tablespoon of bitters and one tablespoon of sugar syrup. Strain and serve. A **Rob Roy** – not to be confused with the Scotch whisky brand of that name – is much the same: use half Scotch to half Italian Vermouth, and a dash of Angostura.

Blue Blazer. Warm a generous measure of whisky and pour it into a flame-proof tankard or mug. Set light to the contents. When the flames die down, top up with boiling water, add a twist of lemon peel and stir in two teaspoonsful of honey until it has dissolved.

Highland Coffee. Not as famous, perhaps, as *Irish Coffee* but there's really no reason why a smoky Scotch whisky should not be used. All you need to make this is Scotch whisky, hot ground coffee (not instant), brown sugar and cream. How much Scotch whisky you use is a matter of taste but the art of making a good whisky coffee is to produce a mixture which has a distinctive taste of its own while still allowing you to savour the individual ingredients. Once

whisky, coffee and sugar have been mixed together, only then add the cream by floating it onto the surface of the drink using the back of a spoon. Do not mix the cream into the whisky coffee, but drink the hot, potent liquid through the cooling cream – a marvellous sensation!

Scotch and . . .

Soda. How much of each you use is a matter of taste. You can buy soda water, which is fizzy, in bottles or syphons. Scotch and soda has a long pedigree, harking back to the brandy and soda days of the 19th century – then the English

Left: *Whisky Mac.* Above: *The Wembley – Scotch, Vermouth and pineapple juice – the cocktail with a kick in it!*

gentleman's favourite tipple. More recently, some people are turning to sparking mineral waters as an alternative to soda water.
Lemonade. A popular drink in Scotland. For anyone with a sweet tooth, this could be for you!
Ginger. There are different types of ginger ale, but all should have a slight spicy taste. **Scotch Horse's Neck** comprises Scotch whisky, ginger ale, lemon juice and Angostura.

A Chronology of Events

1494: Oldest reference to whisky, in the Scottish Exchequer Rolls as 'aquavitae'.

1618: 'Uiskie' mentioned in the funeral account of a Highland laird.

1707: Treaty of Union which combined the English and Scottish parliaments into that of the United Kingdom.

1713: British Parliament imposes a proportion of the English malt tax in Scotland and the great age of illicit stills and smuggling begins.

1715: First Jacobite rebellion under the Old Pretender.

1719: General Wade begins building roads for use in controlling the Highlands.

1745: Second Jacobite rebellion under Bonnie Prince Charlie.

1746: Battle of Culloden Moor; Bonnie Prince Charlie defeated.

1773: Johnson and Boswell's tour to the Hebrides.

1800: Matthew Gloag, of The Famous Grouse fame, opens a grocery and wine merchants business in Perth and starts dealing in whiskies.

1815: Charles Mackinlay sets up business in Leith.

1820: John Walker buys a grocery, wine and spirit business in Kilmarnock.

1822: King George IV pays a state visit to Scotland; he is presented with some illicitly distilled The Glenlivet.

1823: A new Act of Parliament makes legal distilling a reasonable proposition for many Highlanders.

1824: George Smith of The Glenlivet takes out a licence under the new Act and builds a new distillery; John Haig builds a distillery at Cameron Bridge.

1825: Arthur Bell and Sons founded in Perth.

1830: Invention of a patent still by the exciseman Aeneas Coffey, used in the production of grain whisky.

1845: John Begg acquires lease of part of the Lochnagar mountain near Balmoral Castle, from where he produced 'Royal' Lochnagar single malt whisky.

1846: John Dewar and Sons founded.

1860: The Excise permits the blending of whiskies from different distilleries, thus making way for the emergence of distinctive brands of blended whisky.

1863: William Sanderson Ltd., of Vat 69 fame, founded.

1877: Six Lowland patent still distillers combine to form Distillers Company Ltd.

1880s: Production of cognac in France devastated by deadly *phylloxera* insect, creating a gap in the English market which Scotch whisky fills.

1883: 'White Horse Distillers Ltd.' founded by James Logan Mackie in Glasgow.

1886: William Grant buys surplus plant from the Cardhu Distillery and begins building the Glenfiddich distillery; 'Whisky Tom' Dewar exhibits his whiskies at a brewer's show at the Agricultural Hall in Islington.

1895: Gordon and MacPhail, independent bottlers, founded in Elgin.

1898: Bankruptcy of Pattison's Ltd., a major blender and wholesale merchant, ruining a number of distilling firms and forcing others to launch export drives to sell surplus stock.

1905: London Borough of Islington takes out summonses as test cases against certain publicans for selling 'adulterated' whisky.

1908: Royal Commission set up to determine what is whisky.

1914-18: The First World War; distilling is restricted and spirits rationed.

1915: As a wartime measure, whisky for consumption in Britain has to be matured for three years – this minimum period remains.

1917: John Alexander Dewar becomes Baron Forteviot of Dupplin.

1919: Tommy Dewar gets his peerage – Baron Dewar of Homestall, Sussex.

1920: Prohibition in the U.S.A.

1922: James Buchanan, producer of 'Black & White' whisky, becomes Baron Woolavington of Lavington.

1929: Wall Street crash and subsequent depression brings down the whisky distilleries of Campbeltown.

1933: Prohibition era in the U.S.A comes to an end; some brands of Scotch whisky such as Berry Bros and Rudd's Cutty Sark make their reputation during this period.

1939-45: The Second World War brings cutbacks in production and rationing of Scotch whisky.

1950: The Canadian company, Seagram, buys Chivas Brothers and expands its foothold in Scotch whisky.

1954: Restrictions on releases of Scotch whisky in the U.K. end.

1985: Guinness plc acquires Arthur Bell and Sons.

1986: Guinness plc takes over the Distillers Company Ltd. to become the biggest name in Scotch whisky.

Glossary

Barrel. A cask containing approximately 180 litres (40 gals.).

Burnt ale. The liquor left in the wash still after the first distillation in the pot still process. Also known as **pot ale.**

Butt. A cask containing approximately 500 litres (110 gals.).

Blended whisky. A combination of mature whiskies from several different distilleries, malt as well as grain.

Coffey still. Used in the production of grain whisky. Also known as a **patent still.**

Diastase. An enzyme secreted by the barley during germination.

Feints. The last runnings of the distillate received from the second distillation in the pot still process.

Fillings. New whisky.

Foreshots. The first runnings of the distillate received from the second distillation in the pot still process. What follows is the potable spirit until the feints are reached.

Grain whisky. Made from malted barley together with unmalted barley and maize, in a continuous process in a patent or Coffey still.

Green malt. Barley which has been allowed to germinate, but still has to be dried.

Heart of the run. That fraction of the distillate received from the second distillation in the pot still process, which is considered to be of the required strength and quality for malt whisky. Also known as the **middle cut.**

Hogshead. A cask containing approximately 250 litres (55 gals.).

Low wines. The name given to the product of the first distillation in the pot still process. It forms the raw material of the second distillation, which is carried out in the spirit still.

Malt whisky. Made from malted barley only, using the pot still process.

Malting. Barley prepared by steeping, germination and drying.

Mash tun. A large circular vessel in which the cereals are mixed with hot water.

Middle cut. See **Heart of the run.**

Patent still. See **Coffey still.**

Peat-reek. To impart to the drying malted barley the desired degree of smokiness.

Pot ale. See **Burnt ale.**

Pot still. A large copper vessel used in distillation, and from which the pot still process derives its name.

Single whisky. The product of one distillery.

Spirit safe. Enables the stillman to test the spirit as it flows from the still.

Spirit still. A pot still used in the second distillation in the pot still process.

Steeps. Tanks of water in which barley is soaked before being allowed to germinate.

Ullage. Spirit lost by evaporation during maturation.

Vatting. Combining malt with malt or grain with grain.

Wash. A weak form of alcohol obtained by fermenting wort with yeast. It is the wash which forms the raw material of the first distillation in the pot still process and of the only distillation in the patent still process.

Washbacks. Large vessels in which the wort is fermented by yeast.

Worm. Together with its surrounding bath of cold running water or **worm-tub**, it forms the condenser unit in the pot still process. The worm is a coiled copper tube of decreasing diameter and in it the vapours from the still condense. It is being gradually replaced by the tubular condenser.

Wort. A sugary liquid drawn off from the mash-tun after mashing the cereals with hot water. In malt distilleries the cereals (barley only) are all malted; in grain distilleries a proportion only is malted, the rest being unmalted.

DIRECTORY OF BRANDS

Using the Directory

Some malts in the directory are unavailable as brands from their distillers, but can be bought from independent bottlers such as Gordon and MacPhail of Elgin and William Cadenhead of Campbeltown (note that Gordon and MacPhail may give the year of distillation rather than the age when bottled).

With blended whisky, it is vitally important that the drink has a consistency and character of its own. Blenders also place great importance on creating a drink which is 'milder' than some malts in order to appeal to a broader range of people. To this end, they are seeking to create a blend which is both smooth and mellow. These characteristics can be more or less assumed with the blended whiskies in this directory.

Where appropriate, I have mentioned that a distillery is open to the public. At some of these distilleries, the opening times may be seasonal, such as during the summer months, while some may allow visitors only by appointment. Check with the distillery beforehand if you are planning a visit – the addresses are given in the directory.

Information on the brands, including remarks on flavour, has come from a variety of sources. A detailed questionnaire was sent to scores of distilleries and whisky companies, and I warmly thank all those who co-operated. The brands in this directory represent a good cross-section of Scotch whisky today. Household names are included but there are a fair number of not-so familiar brands that illuminate the diversity and resourcefulness of the Scotch whisky industry.

SINGLE MALTS

Aberlour

Producing region: Highland.
Age: 12 years old.
Address: Aberlour-Glenlivet Distillery Company, Aberlour, Banffshire.
Parent company: Pernod Ricard.
Available in the U.K. in public houses and shops; its most important export market is France.

The distillery is situated at the foot of Ben Rinnes near where the Lour Burn joins the River Spey. The present distillery was founded in 1879 on the site of an earlier one but since then it has been extensively modernized. The distillery is open to the public.

Aromatic, smooth. Recommended as an after-dinner drink.

Ardbeg

Producing region: Islay.
Age: 10 years old.
Address: Ardbeg Distillery, Port Ellen, Islay.
Parent company: Hiram Walker and Sons (Scotland) plc.

The distillery was established on the south-east coast of the island of Islay in 1815. Before that it had been the haunt of a notorious gang of smugglers. The excisemen seized a large quantity of the illicit whisky during the gang's absence, which led to the gang's break-up and the founding of legitimate distilling operations. Local peat and water drawn from Loch Arinambeast and Uigedale are used in the production.

Smoky, peaty, full-bodied, lingering taste, malty. Recommended with water.

Auchentoshan
(pronounced Och'n'tosh'n)

Producing region: Lowland.
Age: 5, 8, 10, 12, 18 years old. 21 years old to be introduced in 1987.
Address: Auchentoshan Distillery, Dalmuir, near Glasgow.
Parent company: Stanley P. Morrison Ltd.
Available in U.K. bars, restaurants and from spirit retailers; introduced into U.K. duty-free shops in 1986; exported to all E.E.C. countries, the U.S.A., Canada, New Zealand, Japan and Hong Kong.

Auchentoshan means 'corner of the field' in Gaelic. The distillery, which is one of the oldest licensed distilleries in Scotland, was built in 1823. It was bought by Stanley P. Morrison in 1984. It is an unusual malt in that it is triple-distilled. The producers claim that as a result, it is a milder,

Aultmore means 'big burn' in Gaelic. The distillery began producing whisky in 1897. It drew its flavour from the springs on the neighbouring hill and the peat deposits of the Foggie Moss, an area popular with illicit distillers in the early part of the 19th century. In 1952 the distillery was the pilot plant used by Scottish Malt Distillers, a subsidiary of the Distillers Company, to develop the method of turning the waste from malt whisky production into high-protein animal feed. It also remains an essential ingredient of many blends.

Delicate, mellow, smooth.

Balblair

Producing region: Highland.
Age: 5 years.
Address: George Ballantine and Son Ltd., 3 High Street, Dumbarton.
Parent company: Hiram Walker and Sons (Scotland) plc.
Available in Italy.

The present distillery was built in 1790 on the site of a distillery founded in 1749. It lies within a quarter of a mile of the Dornoch Firth near Tain in Ross and Cromarty. The nature of the area explains its distilling advantages: all local streams provide excellent water running through peat. This brand is unusually young for a malt.

Delicate, refreshing, clean taste, smooth, medium-bodied. Pale colour.

The Balvenie Founder's Reserve
(pronounced Balvenny)

Producing region: Highland.
Age: 8–9 years old.
Address: William Grant and Sons Ltd., The Balvenie Distillery, Dufftown, Banffshire.
Available in the U.K. from spirit retailers; Germany, Holland, New Zealand as well as duty-free shops.

The distillery was built in 1892 by William Grant of Glenfiddich fame, using the buildings of New Balvenie Castle as its nucleus. He had bought

the land and the buildings on it to protect the source of the water he used for Glenfiddich and the same spring, the Robbie Dubh, was used for Balvenie. Nearby were the ruins of the original Balvenie Castle, roofless since 1742. Here the Fair Maid of Galloway wed two of the swashbuckling Black Douglases. The first was murdered and the second routed in battle in 1455 by King James II of Scotland. The king was so taken with the Fair Maid's beauty that he reinstated her in Balvenie Castle for the annual rent of a single red rose. The rose symbol is shown on the bottle label of the distillery's other brand, The Balvenie Classic.

Sweet, mellow, full-bodied, smooth and rounded. Recommended as an after-dinner drink.

more quickly maturing malt than most and can be bottled at 5 years, as well as the better-known ages of 8, 10 and 12 years. Auchentoshan has received several awards and is rated highly by connoisseurs. The distillery is open to the public.

Delicate, mellow, light-bodied, clean taste, smooth. Pale colour.

Aultmore

Producing region: Highland.
Age: 'over 12 years old'.
Address: Aultmore Distillery, Keith, Banffshire.
Parent company: Guinness plc.
Available in the U.K., France, Germany, U.S.A., Canada and Australia.

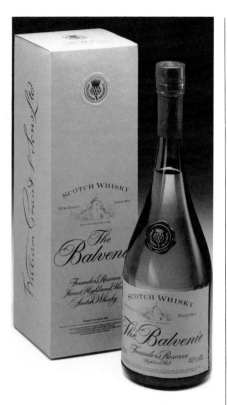

roofed kiln. It was eventually acquired by The Seagram Company Ltd. in 1978. Benriach is mainly used for blending but is available from independent bottlers.

Lightly peated, aromatic, light-bodied, smooth. Pale colour.

Benromach

Producing region: Highland.
Age: distilled 1968 and variable vintage ages.
Address: Gordon and MacPhail, 58-60 South Street, Elgin.
Available from U.K. spirit retailers and other specialist outlets; export markets are mainly European. Also available from William Cadenhead Ltd. – see 'De luxe blends'.

Delicate, light-bodied.

Bladnoch

Producing region: Lowland.
Age: 'minimum eight years old'.
Address: Arthur Bell and Sons plc, Cherrybank, Perth.
Parent company: Guinness plc.
Exported to most world markets.

Bladnoch is located at Wigtown in Galloway. It is Scotland's most southerly distillery.

Sweet, smooth. Recommend as a pre-dinner drink.

Blair Athol

Producing region: Highland.
Age: 'minimum 8 years old'.
Address: Blair Athol Distillery, Pitlochry, Perthshire.
Parent company: Guinness plc.

Benriach

Producing region: Highland.
Age: distilled 1969 and variable vintage ages.
Address: Benriach Distillery, Elgin, Moray.
Parent Company: The Seagram Company Ltd.
Available from U.K. spirit retailers and other specialist shops; mainly European export markets. Also available from William Cadenhead.

The distillery was built by John Duff south of Elgin in 1897 and acquired by the neighbouring Longmorn distillery in 1901. It was re-built in the 1960s with the resurgence in demand for Scotch whisky, but still has its working floor-maltings and pagoda-

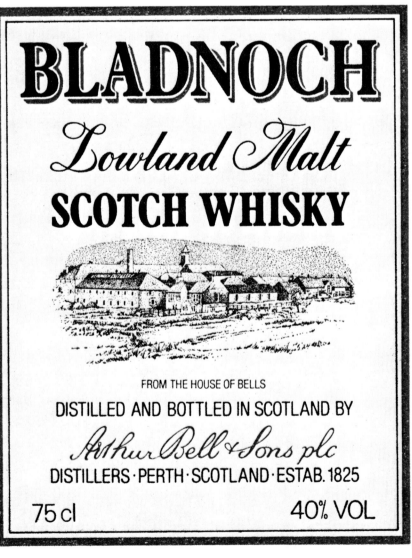

BLADNOCH
Lowland Malt
SCOTCH WHISKY

FROM THE HOUSE OF BELLS

DISTILLED AND BOTTLED IN SCOTLAND BY

Arthur Bell & Sons plc
DISTILLERS · PERTH · SCOTLAND · ESTAB. 1825

75 cl   40% VOL

Available widely in the U.K. and abroad.

The distillery was licensed in 1825, although it is thought that whisky was being produced there prior to that date. Arthur Bell and Sons bought in is 1933. The distillery is very picturesque, with its gardens of rhododendrons and roses. The distillery is open to the public.

Smoky, light-bodied. Recommended with or without water as a pre-dinner drink.

Bowmore

Producing region: Islay.
Age: 12 years old.
Address: Bowmore Distillery, Bowmore, Islay.
Parent company: Stanley P. Morrison Ltd.
Available in U.K. duty-free shops, bars, restaurants and from spirit retailers. Exported to all E.E.C. countries, the U.S.A., Canada,

Scandinavia, Switzerland, Japan, Australia, New Zealand, Hong Kong and South Africa; and available in duty-free shops in Denmark, Italy, Australia and Japan.

Bowmore Distillery was founded in 1779 and thus has a claim to being among the oldest legal distilleries on the island. In 1790 a parish minister wrote that the island had 'a liberty of brewing whisky, without being under the necessity of paying the usual excise duty to the government'

– a privilege long since gone. Bowmore is one of the few distilleries which retains the traditional floor method of malting barley. Over a hundred years ago Bowmore was sold with the motto, *Fioghinn agus Soir Bhuanaghadh* which is Islay Gaelic for 'full and excellent quality'.

Smoky, peaty, full-bodied, smooth. Amber colour. Recommended with a splash of water as an after-dinner drink.

Bruichladdich
(pronounced Bru-ik-laddy)

Producing region: Islay.
Age: 10 years old.
Address: Bruichladdich, Islay.
Parent company: The Invergordon Distillers (Holdings) Ltd.
Available in the U.K. Exported worldwide.

The distillery is in a beautiful setting on the western shore of Loch Indaal on Islay – going west the next distillery you come to is in America! The name means the 'hill on the shore' in Gaelic. The distillery went into production in 1881 and some of the original equipment such as the wash tun brewing tank is still in use. It is one of the few Scottish distilleries to have riveted stills. Water is drawn from the hills behind the distillery.

Peaty, lingering taste, smooth. Golden colour.

"Westering Home"...

Bunnahabhain

SINGLE MALT SCOTCH WHISKY

PRODUCT OF SCOTLAND

DISTILLED AND BOTTLED BY THE HIGHLAND DISTILLERIES COMPANY plc
BUNNAHABHAIN DISTILLERY ISLE OF ISLAY SCOTLAND

40% vol.   75cl

Bunnahabhain

(pronounced Bunnaharvin)

Producing region: Islay.
Age: 12 years old.
Address: Bunnahabhain Distillery, Port Askaig, Islay.
Parent company: The Highland Distilleries Co. plc.
Available in all types of U.K. outlets; in the U.S.A., France, Germany, Italy, South Africa, Holland, Belgium, Canada, Australia, Japan, Scandinavia.

The distillery, the most northerly on Islay, was brought on stream in 1883 by the Greenlees brothers, both local farmers, to make use of their grain. The name translates as 'mouth of the river' – the distillery is near the mouth of the river Margadale which flows into the Sound of Islay. In 1887, the Islay Distillery Company, which had begun building Bunnahabhain six years earlier, amalgamated with Glenrothes-Glenlivet to form the Highland Distilleries Co. A publication of the 1880s describes how the distillery had been provided with a good road, a handsome pier and a reading room and school room for the workmen's children. The sense of community that grew up around the distillery remains today. The distillery is open to the public.

The most lightly peated and delicate of the Islay malts, with a smooth, well-rounded flavour. Mellow. Dark in colour. Recommended 'all the time with anything'.

Caol Ila

(pronounced Caol-eela)

Producing region: Islay.
Age: distilled 1969 and variable vintage ages.
Address: Gordon and MacPhail, 58-60 South Street, Elgin.
Available from U.K. spirit retailers and other specialist outlets; various export markets, mainly European.

Caol Ila means the 'Sound of Islay' and is the Gaelic for the strait that separates the island of Islay from the island of Jura on the west coast of Scotland. The distillery, which lies by the sea, was acquired by Bulloch Lade in 1857 and extended and improved by them in 1879. The distillery draws its water from the Loch Nam Bam 'over which ever and anon the fragrant breeze from the myrtle and blooming heather is wafted' (Alfred Barnard, 1887). Caol Ila, as well as being available from the independent bottlers, is also an essential ingredient in the 'BL' Gold Label and Old Rarity blends.

Peaty, tangy.

Caperdonich

Producing region: Highland.
Age: distilled 1968 and variable vintage ages.
Address: Caperdonich Distillery, Rothes, Moray.
Parent Company: The Seagram Company Ltd.
Available from U.K. spirit retailers and other specialist outlets; mainly European export markets. Also available from William Cadenhead.

The distillery draws water from the Caperdonich or 'secret well' – on Speyside. It was founded in 1897 by Major James Grant, of Glen Grant fame, but closed in 1901. It was reconstructed and re-opened by The Glenlivet and Glen Grant Distilleries Ltd. in 1965 as a small, highly-automated efficient distillery. The distillery became part of The Seagram Company Ltd. in 1978 and is well-known for its blending qualities.

Sweet, light-bodied, dry.
Recommended as an after-dinner drink.

Cardhu

Producing region: Highland.
Age: 12 years old.
Address: Cardhu Distillery, Knockando, Aberlour, Banffshire.
Parent company: Guinness plc.
Available from all types of U.K. outlets; exported worldwide.

The distillery is situated on Speyside in a remote area which afforded the first distillers there a degree of protection from the attentions of the excisemen. Its name is Gaelic – it was previously anglicized to Cardow – and means 'black rock', referring to the neighbouring Mannoch Hills which are the source of the distillery's spring water. John Cumming took a lease out on Cardow Farm in 1811 and five years later, was convicted on three occasions for distilling without a licence.

Women have played a particularly important role at Cardhu. According to local tradition, it was John Cumming's wife Helen who did the brewing, and in her capacity to thwart the Excise, no one was equal to her. Stories abound about her: one of the best concerns the day that she was visited by one of the fairies of Sheean o' Mannoch, the fairy hillocks around Knockando! Helen gave the shivering creature some of her whisky. The fairy drained it and said: 'Brew, wifie, brew, for you and yours will never want'. John Cumming's son Lewis gave his chief attention to making superior whisky, priding himself that Cardhu was then the smallest distillery in Scotland. It was not until his shrewd wife Elizabeth took over on his death that the distillery was re-built and its capacity increased. She was the only woman to work a distillery at that time. In 1893, John Walker and Sons Ltd., who along with other blenders needed to secure a good source of supply, bought the distillery from Mrs Cumming, but her son John was retained as distillery manager and was appointed a director of Walker's.

Cardhu is a key ingredient of the Johnnie Walker blends. The distillery is open to the public.

Clean taste, delicate, smooth, mellow. Pale colour. Recommended with or without water as an after-dinner drink.

Clynelish

(pronounced Clyneleesh)

Producing region: Highland.
Age: 12 years old.
Address: Clynelish, Brora, Sutherland.
Parent company: Guinness plc.

The distillery was established in 1819 by the Marquess of Stafford who had married the heiress of the vast Sutherland estates and took that name when he was made a duke. He became infamous for his part in the Highland Clearances and his statue at Ben Bhraggie has been referred to as a 'monument to misery'. Between 1809 and 1819, 15,000 crofters were cleared from nearly half a million acres by the Marquess and those who did not emigrate were moved to the seaboard. The Clynelish distillery fitted into a plan for regenerating arable farms on the coastal strip. As was so often the case, the Clynelish farm was let to a Mr. Harper from the Lowlands, who also erected a distillery. It was hoped he would provide the smaller tenants with a market for their grain so that they wouldn't go to an illicit distiller, and illicit distilling would then die out.

Although a very early 'purpose-built' distillery, it was still well-integrated with its farm: grains left over from manufacturing fed the farm pigs whose manure was used to reclaim part of the Brora Muir. Coal from the mine at Brora – the duke sunk a fresh shaft – was used in the distillery's furnaces. Clynelish was enlarged by those who followed Harper. In 1925, the Distillers Company Ltd. acquired all the shares in the distillery. Clynelish was closed during the Depression and war years. In the 1960s a new distillery, named Clynelish, was built on an adjacent site. (In 1975, the old distillery was re-opened as Brora Distillery.) The distillery is open to the public.

Dry. Recommended as an after-dinner drink.

Craigellachie

Producing region: Highland.
Age: distilled 1971 and other vintage ages.
Address: Gordon and MacPhail, 58-60 South Street, Elgin.
Also available from William Cadenhead Ltd. – see 'De luxe blends'.

The Craigellachie Distillery Company Ltd. was founded in 1888 on a spur of a hill overlooking the village of Craigellachie, the precipitous Rock of Craigellachie, the winding River Spey and Telford's iron bridge of 1815. The man who dominated the distillery was Peter Mackie of White Horse fame. From 1900 he chaired the annual general meetings at Craigellachie, using them as a platform for his strongly-held opinions on the whisky industry, the nation and the British Empire!

'Restless Peter' believed in exact planning, hard work and rigid discipline – all illustrated by the massive movement he organized in 1922 of 2,300 casks from Craigellachie to warehouses he had bought in Campbeltown. This entailed chartering special trains from Craigellachie to Lossiemouth – running two or three times per day for four days in all – and two steamers which sailed round the north of Scotland to the Mull of Kintyre. In 1923 a visitor to Craigellachie noted the carefully-tended gardens and trim little cottages of the distillery employees. There was, in fact, an annual inspection of the gardens by the directors, followed by a presentation of prizes for those that were kept the best – a fine illustration of Mackie's close involvement in Craigellachie.

Smoky, delicate, aromatic, light-bodied. Recommended as an after-dinner drink.

Dallas Dhu

Producing region: Highland.
Age: distilled 1969 and variable vintage ages.
Address: Gordon and MacPhail, 58-60 South Street, Elgin.
Available from U.K. spirit retailers and other specialist outlets; various export markets – mainly European. Also available from William Cadenhead Ltd. – see 'De luxe blends'.

Not the favourite tipple of J.R. Ewing! Dallas Dhu takes its name from the Gaelic Dalais Dubh, meaning 'black water valley'.

Dalmore

Producing region: Highland.
Age: 12 years old.
Address: Whyte and Mackay Distillers, Dalmore House, 296-8 St. Vincent Street, Glasgow.
Parent company: Lonrho plc.
Available in U.K. public houses, specialist retailers, some supermarkets; in France, Italy, Portugal and Korea in particular, and duty-free outlets.

The first Dalmore whisky ran into oak casks in 1839. In early times there were only two stills, but today eight stills produce up to 65,000 litres (14,300 gals) of alcohol each week and there are warehouses for 15 million litres (3.3 million gals).

Sherried, mellow, full-bodied, lingering taste, round. Deep, rich golden colour. Recommended as an after-dinner drink.

Dalwhinnie

Producing region: Highland.
Age: 18 years old.
Address: Dalwhinnie Distillery, Dalwhinnie, Inverness-shire.
Parent company: Guinness plc.

Dalwhinnie means 'meeting place' in Gaelic. The distillery was built in the 1890s at a crossroads for cattle drovers and, in previous times, whisky smugglers. The desolate area around

the distillery is steeped in the lore of the '45 and Bonnie Prince Charlie is held to have taken refuge in the nearby 'Prince Charlie's Cave' after the battle of Culloden.

Recommended as a pre-dinner malt.

Deanston Malt

Producing region: Highland.
Age: 8 years old.
Address: Deanston Distillers Ltd. 9/21 Salamander Place, Leith, Edinburgh.
Parent company: The Invergordon Distillers Holdings Ltd.
Available in the U.K. Exported worldwide.

The distillery was established first as a mill on the banks of the River Teith in Perthshire in 1785. Near the distillery lies Castle Doune, the setting of an old Scottish ballad lamenting the slaying of the young and gallant Earl of Moray, a favourite of Mary Queen of Scots.

Mellow, light-bodied, clean taste. Golden colour.

Dufftown

Producing region: Highland.
Age: 'minimum 8 years'.
Address: Dufftown-Glenlivet Distillery, Dufftown, Banffshire.
Parent company: Guinness plc. Available widely in the U.K. and abroad.

The distillery was established in 1896 and bought from the firm of Peter Mackenzie by Bell's in 1933. Bell's also bought up surrounding land including the Pittyvaich Farm where they built a new malt distillery in 1973. The Dufftown-Glenlivet distillery draws its water from Jock's Well in the Conval Hills. The Dullan Water provides power as it did for the saw and meal mills previously on this spot.

Well-rounded flavour. Recommended with or without water as a pre-dinner drink.

Glen Albyn

Producing region: Highland.
Age: distilled 1963 and variable vintage ages.
Address: Gordon and MacPhail, 58-60 South Street, Elgin. Available from U.K. spirit retailers and other specialist outlets; mainly European export markets. Available also from William Cadenhead Ltd. – see 'De luxe blends'.

The distillery lies near Glen Mhor distillery, near Inverness.

Glenburgie

Producing region: Highland.
Address: James and George Stodart Ltd., 3 High Street, Dumbarton.
Parent company: Hiram Walker and Sons (Scotland) plc.

Built near Forres in 1810 by William Paul on the estate of the Cumyn family, this distillery has in its vicinity a druid temple beside a lovely loch near the desolate scene of Macbeth's legendary meeting with the witches 'so wither'd, and so wild in their attire'.

Glendullan

Producing region: Highland.
Age: 12 years old.
Address: Glendullan, Dufftown, Banffshire.
Parent company: Guinness plc. Export markets are the U.S.A., Europe, Africa and South America.

Rarely seen in the U.K.

Mellow, aromatic, lingering taste, smooth. Recommended as an after-dinner drink.

Glen Elgin

Producing region: Highland.
Age: 12 years old.
Address: Glen Elgin Distillery, Longmorn, Elgin.
Parent company: Guinness plc.

This was one of the last distilleries to be built in the boom preceding the crash of Pattison's Ltd., and was designed by Charles Doig of Elgin, architect of many distilleries. He predicted at the time that it would be the last to be put up on Speyside for 50 years – he was proved right. In 1964 Glen Elgin was considerably re-built and re-equipped.

Sweet, aromatic.

Glenesk

Producing region: Highland.
Age: 12 years old.

Address: Glen Esk Distillery, Hillside, Montrose.
Parent company: Guinness plc.

Located on the east coast of Scotland, it was at one time converted to grain whisky production.

Delicate, full-bodied. Recommended as an after-dinner drink.

Glenfarclas

Producing region: Highland.
Age: 8, 12, 15, 21 and 25 years old.

Address: J. and G. Grant, Glenfarclas Distillery, Marypark, Ballindalloch, Banffshire.
Available in the U.K. from public houses, from spirit retailers and specialist stores. Its export markets are France, other European countries and North America.

This independent, family-owned dis-tillery celebrated its 150th anniver-sary in 1986 and is headed by a managing director, John Grant, who is the great, great grandson of the founder, John Grant. Glenfarclas means 'glen of the green grassland' and it was with the object of using Glenfarclas as a staging post between his cattle, horse and sheep farms and the market in Elgin that John Grant negotiated a tenancy agreement in 1856. The agreement included the farm distillery, but it was not until 1870 that the Grants took over the running of the distillery themselves. The distillery suffered badly from the Pattison crash – Pattison's Ltd. had a 50 per cent share – but by the late 1920s it was prospering again and began bottling its whisky and export-ing to the U.S.A. The distillery is open to the public.

Sherried, full-bodied, lingering taste, smooth. Dark in colour.

Glenfarclas 105

Producing region: Highland.
Age: 8 years old.
Address: J. and G. Grant, Glenfarclas Distillery, Marypark, Ballindalloch, Banffshire.
Available in the U.K. in public houses, from spirit retailers and specialist stores; exported to Canada, Germany, France, Australia, Belgium, Holland, Switzerland, Italy and Denmark.

Glenfarclas 105 is malt whisky at cask strength – 60 per cent volume. It is among the strongest bottled malt whiskies available. The distillery is open to the public.

Sherried, full-bodied, lingering taste, smooth. Dark colour. Recommended as an after-dinner drink. Dilute to taste!

Glenfiddich

Producing region: Highland.
Age: 'at least 8 years (some 12 years)'.
Address: The Glenfiddich Distillery, Dufftown, Banffshire.
Parent company: William Grant and Sons Ltd.
Widely available in the U.K. It has 186 export markets throughout the world.

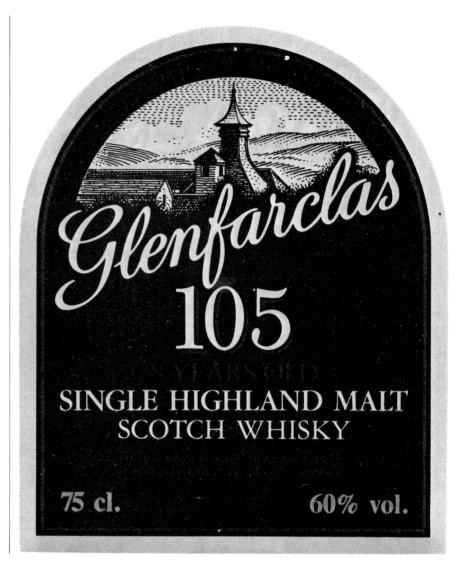

Today Glenfiddich is the world's leading Scotch malt whisky. It is fitting that its history should be in the best tradition of the Highlands. Its founder, William Grant, was a hard-working and canny Highlander who, with the help of a large and loyal family, literally built the business with his own bare hands. He was born in 1839 to a poor tailor and veteran of the Battle of Waterloo, but by 1866 he had raised himself to manager of the Mortlach Distillery in his home town of Dufftown. In 1870, after a fruitless venture in quarry-lime, Grant resolved to make his fortune in the 'Great Adventure' as he called it, of whisky distilling. Every penny the family could save – his wife from stringent home economies, himself from his distillery salary and earnings as a precentor of the Free Church of Dufftown, his growing children from their university prizes and, in the case of his eldest son John, a teaching salary – was put into a fund for the building of a distillery.

In 1886, after years of saving, Grant seized upon a piece of luck. It had been decided at the nearby Cardhu Distillery at Knockando to install new plant and Grant was able to buy the old plant at a knockdown price of £119.19.0d. Grant chose a spot for his distillery on the slopes of the Conval Hills using water from the Robbie Dubh spring and harnessing the power of the Fiddich river below to drive the plant. With the help of only one mason and carpenter, Grant and his family built their own distillery for a little over £700, and began distilling. They worked seven days a week, the children studying while watching over the plant, and the first whisky ran from the still on Christmas Day 1887. It was not in Grant's nature to haggle over prices and at first he had problems selling his whisky. Then Smith's Glenlivet Distillery caught fire and Grant was able to step in and meet an order for whisky fillings that Smith's was unable to meet. The distillery prospered and in 1892 Grant built a second at Balvenie. The Grant family survived the spectactular crash of the Pattison family in 1898 which led to unsaleable surplus stocks of whisky, by expanding from being purely distillers to wholesalers and blenders who supplied the retailers direct, and by exporting overseas. The distillery is open to the public.

Light-bodied, smooth, dry, fragrant, distinctive, fresh. Pale colour.

Glen Garioch
(pronounced Glengeerie)

Producing region: Highland
Age: 10 years old. 21 years old planned for this year (1987).
Address: Glengarioch Distillery, Oldmeldrum, Aberdeenshire.
Parent company: Stanley P. Morrison Ltd.
Available from U.K. spirit retailers, bars and restaurants; in all E.E.C. countries, the U.S.A. and Australia.

Glengarioch Distillery, a timeless cluster of grey granite buildings in

the village of Oldmeldrum, near Aberdeen, has been producing malt whisky since 1797. The barley is still malted at the distillery and germination is controlled by hand and eye. The distillery used to close down in the summer months when cooling was expensive and the men of Oldmeldrum were needed to work in the granite quarry. Today the distillery operates all year round. New techniques in the recycling of waste heat have won the distillery recog-

nition from the Department of Energy who have nominated the latest installation as a demonstration project. Part of the reclaimed heat is used in the distillery itself, but the remainder is used in glasshouses which produce 150 tons of tomatoes a year – and very nice they are, too!

Peaty, full bodied, lingering taste, smooth, malty. Pale in colour.
Recommended as an after-dinner drink.

Glenglassaugh

(*pronounced Glenglassoch*)

Producing region: Highland.
Age: distilled 1967 and variable vintage ages.
Address: Gordon and MacPhail, 58–60 South Street, Elgin.
Available from U.K. spirit retailers and other specialist shops; mainly European export markets.

The distillery was built near the Banffshire fishing town of Portsoy famous for the marble which was used at Versailles.

Medium/full-bodied.

Glengoyne

Producing region: Highland.
Age: 10, 12 and 17 years old.
Address: Glengoyne Distillery, Dumgoyne, Stirlingshire.
Parent company: Robertson and Baxter Ltd.
Available from U.K. spirit retailers and on licensed premises; widely exported, particularly the U.S.A. and Italy.

Glengoyne Distillery is located in a beautiful setting in a wooded glen at the foot of Dumgoyne Hill in the Campsie Hills, Stirlingshire. It was in this area that Rob Roy McGregor, immortalized by Sir Walter Scott, did his cattle thieving and only yards from the distillery lies the stump of an oak tree, said to have been one of his hiding places. In 1876 Lang Brothers Ltd., the wine and spirit merchants, bought Glengoyne which was further extended and modernized after Lang's was acquired by Robertson and Baxter Ltd. Glengoyne 10 years old is at the heart of the Lang's blends. The distillery is open to the public.

Delicate, sweet, mellow, smooth, medium-bodied. Dark colour.

Glen Grant

Producing region: Highland.
Age: U.K. market – no age stated, export – 5, 10 and no age.
Address: Glen Grant Distillery, Rothes, Morayshire.
Parent company: The Seagram Company Ltd.
Glen Grant is widely available in the U.K. Exported worldwide.

Glen Grant distillery was established in Rothes by the brothers James and John Grant who are represented in the 'two Highlanders' label. The Grant brothers came from a long line of farmers whose living had long since been supplemented by the illicit production of malt whisky. James Grant became a prominent local businessman and Provost of Elgin. Glen

Grant passed to his son, Major James Grant, in 1897, under whose stewardship Glen Grant reputedly became the first single malt to be sold in bottle outside the locality of the distillery. Major James' grandson, Major Douglas Mackessack, continued to maintain an interest in the distillery which was acquired by the Seagram Company Ltd. in 1978. The distillery uses water from the Back burn and its eight large 'Grant' stills are coal-fired as of old. The distillery is open to the public.

No Age: medium-bodied, malty, smooth, delicate. Pale amber colour.
5 Years Old: light-bodied, dry, malty, aromatic, lingering taste. Pale colour.
10 Years Old: full-bodied, sweet, malty, mellow. Amber colour.

The Glenlivet

Producing region: Highland.
Age: 12 years.

Address: The Glenlivet Distillery, Ballindalloch, Banffshire.
Parent company: The Seagram Company Ltd.

There is only one whisky that can call itself *The* Glenlivet. In 1880 exclusive use of 'The Glenlivet' was secured by John Gordon Smith after he took legal action against other distillers who had been calling their whisky Glenlivet even though their distilleries were not in the glen. The court ruled that only he could use the label The Glenlivet while ten others could hyphenate their names with Glenlivet. But The Glenlivet was famous a long time before it was legalized, and George IV was presented with, and gratefully received some on his state visit to Scotland in 1822.

The first person to take out a licence under the Excise Act of 1823 was George Smith who built the Glenlivet distillery with the encouragement of his landlord, the Duke of Gordon. He came from a family of farmers and

distillers. His grandfather, John Gow, had come to the area after the defeat of Bonnie Prince Charlie, whom he supported, changing his name to John Smith. George Smith was forced to defend his distillery in the face of threats from illicit distillers, but the business prospered and was handed down through the family, including John Gordon Smith. Captain Bill Smith Grant assumed control in 1921 and opened up the American market for The Glenlivet. He guided his company into a merger with the Glen Grant Distillery to form The Glenlivet and Glen Grant Distilleries Ltd. This company merged with Hill Thomson and Company in 1970 to form The Glenlivet Distillers Ltd. which in 1978 became part of The Seagram Company Ltd. The distillery is open to the public.

Delicate, mellow, lingering taste, malty, medium-bodied. Pale amber colour.

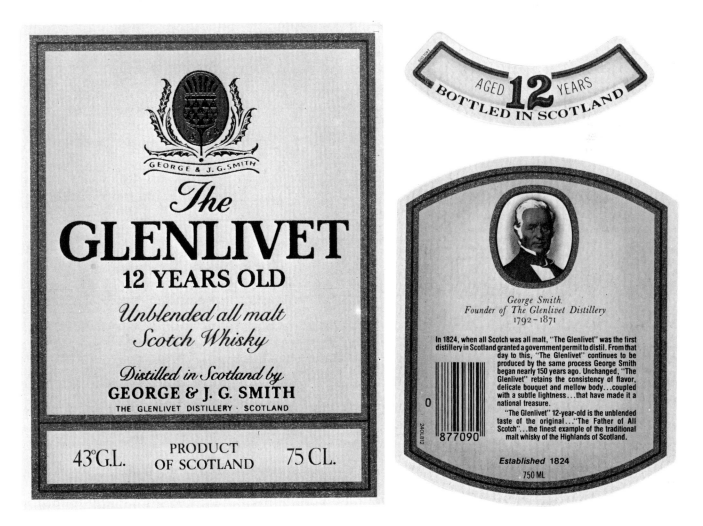

Glen Mhor

Producing region: Highland.
Age: 8 and 15 years old.
Address: Gordon and MacPhail, 58–60 South Street, Elgin.
Available from U.K. spirit retailers and other specialist outlets; mainly European export markets. Also available from William Cadenhead Ltd. – see 'De luxe blends'.

This brand is named after the Mhor or Great Glen in which Loch Ness is to be found. The distillery, in fact, draws its water from Loch Ness and is sited on the banks of the Caledonian Canal to facilitate the transport of grain.

Sweet, light-bodied.

Glenmorangie
(pronounced Glenmorrenjie)

Producing region: Highland.
Age: 10 years old.
Address: The Glenmorangie Distillery Company, Tain, Ross-shire.
Parent company: Macdonald and Muir Ltd.
Available from most U.K. spirit retailers and on licensed premises. It is exported to most world markets from Andorra to Peru.

The distillery is situated on the windswept shores of the Dornoch Firth near Tain in Ross-shire in the far north of Scotland. Glenmorangie is from the Gaelic meaning 'glen of tranquillity' or less eloquently 'the valley of the low ground beside the water'! The distillery was registered in 1843 by a Mr Matheson of Tain, but the site by the old farmhouse of

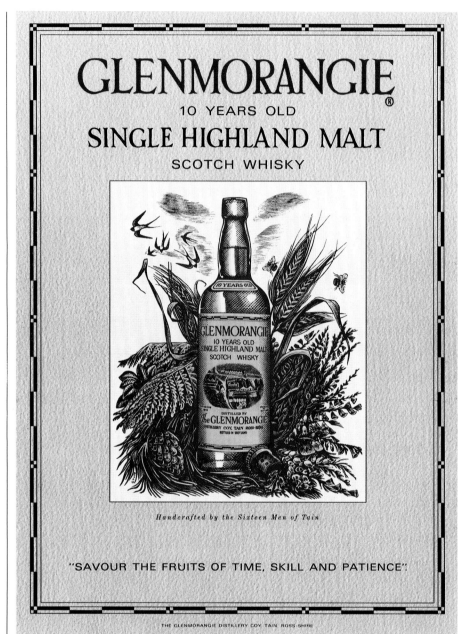

Handcrafted by the Sixteen Men of Tain

"SAVOUR THE FRUITS OF TIME, SKILL AND PATIENCE"

THE GLENMORANGIE DISTILLERY COY. TAIN ROSS-SHIRE

Morangie has been famous for the production of alcohol since 1738.

The distillery has its own water supply, the Tarlogie Springs, which flow through sandstone, and uses local Ross-shire barley. The swannecked stills installed in the 1880s are the highest in the Highlands (5.13m/16ft 10¼ins.), the company claiming that they ensure that only the purest vapours ascend to the top of the neck column. The distillery was purchased by Macdonald and Muir Ltd. in the 1890s. The 16-strong workforce have become known as the Sixteen Men of Tain and are featured individually in the advertising of Glenmorangie. It is used in the Highland Queen blend.

The distillery is open to the public.

Smoky, delicate, sweet, aromatic, light-bodied, smooth. Pale in colour.

Glen Moray

Producing region: Highland.
Age: 12 years old.
Address: The Glen Moray-Glenlivet Distillery Company, Elgin.
Parent company: Macdonald and Muir Ltd.
Available from U.K. spirit retailers and in most world markets, particularly Germany, Italy and North America.

Towser, the distillery cat (1963-1987), was born in the still house and has her name in the *Guinness Book of Records* as the greatest mouser on record; she is recorded as having caught 28,899 mice! The distillery is open to the public.

Mellow, full-bodied, smooth. Very light colour – no colouring added. Normally drunk without water.

Glenugie

Producing region: Highland.
Age: distilled 1966 and variable vintage ages.
Address: Gordon and MacPhail, 58–60 South Street, Elgin.
Available from U.K. spirit retailers and other specialist outlets; mainly European export markets. Also available from William Cadenhead Ltd. – see 'De luxe blends'.

The distillery takes its water from the Ugie burn and, situated near Peterhead, is the most easterly in Scotland. It was built in 1875 and is in the hands of Long John Distillers Ltd. Few convicts have escaped from nearby Peterhead Prison but most come via the distillery as it is the quickest way from the prison into the open country.

Fruity.

The distillery was established two miles west of Elgin in 1897 and bought by Macdonald and Muir Ltd. of Leith who use its malt in their Highland Queen standard blend. The distillery is open to the public.

Delicate, refreshing, clean taste, smooth, medium-bodied. Pale colour.

The Glenturret

Producing region: Highland
Age: 8, 12, 15, 21, 25 years old.
Address: Glenturret, The Hosh, Crieff, Perthshire.
Parent company: Highland Distillers.

Available in the UK from selected outlets; its export markets are in Europe, mainly Germany, Italy, Holland and France.

Glenturret distillery is reputedly the oldest single Highland malt distillery in Scotland. It was established in 1775, but dates back to 1717 when there were numerous illicit stills in Glenturret all drawing their water from the River Turret. In 1921 Glenturret ceased distilling and by 1927 all maturing whisky had been removed from the warehouses. James Fairlie bought the distillery in 1957 and began its revival. It was producing spirit again by 1960. The Glenturret has won many awards.

Glenury-Royal

Producing region: Highland.
Age: 12 years old.
Address: Glenury-Royal Distillery, Stonehaven.
Parent company: Guinness plc.

The distillery was built by Captain Robert Barclay in 1833, a local farmer, MP and celebrated marathon walker.

Smoky, dry, light-bodied.
Recommended as a pre-dinner drink.

Glenvale

Producing region: Highland.
Age: 8 years old.
Address: Clydesdale Scotch Whisky Co Ltd.
Available in the U.S.A.

Mellow, full-bodied, clean taste, smooth, malty. Pale in colour. Recommended with water.

Highland Park

Producing region: Highland.
Age: 12 years old.
Address: Highland Park Distillery, Holm Road, Kirkwall, Orkney.
Parent company: The Highland Distilleries Co. plc.
Available in all types of U.K. outlets; widely exported, especially to France, Italy and Japan.

Highland Park is Scotland's most northerly distillery, sited on a grassy hillside overlooking the sombre waters of Scapa Flow with its naval connections, and Orkney's charming capital Kirkwall with its Viking connections. The present day distillery was established in the 1790s. But distilling on the site dates back much further – on the same spot and using the same water supply, Magnus Eunson, a notorious smuggler, operated his illicit still and lead the excise men a merry dance for a good part of the 18th century. The distillery still does all its own malting by hand. Since 1935, it has been owned by the Highland Distilleries Co. A drink much revered by connoisseurs. The distillery is open to public.

Smoky, full-bodied, aromatic, dry.
Reddish colour. Recommended with water.

Inchgower

Producing region: Highland.
Age: 'at least 12 years old'.
Address: Inchgower Distillery, Buckie, Banffshire.
Parent company: Guinness plc. Available widely in the U.K. and abroad.

The imposing Inchgower distillery was built in 1871, drawing its water from the Hill of Minduff two and a half miles away which had also once provided the fishing town of Buckie with its water supply. Bell's bought the distillery in 1933 which had such extensive bonded warehouses for its production that accommodation was also provided for other distillers in the district. Bell's also converted the distillery from coal to steam power.

Light distinctive taste. Recommended with or without water as an after-dinner drink.

Isle of Jura

Producing region: Highland.
Age: 10 years old.
Address: The Isle of Jura Distillery Co Ltd., Craighouse, Isle of Jura.
Parent company: The Invergordon Distillers Holdings Ltd. Available in U.K. public houses, clubs and hotels and from spirit retailers; exported worldwide.

Strictly speaking, a Highland malt, though the Isle of Jura itself overlooks Islay. The label features the startling Paps of Jura, the island's mountain range. Eric Blair, better known as George Orwell, wrote *Nineteen Eighty Four* on Jura.

Delicate, mellow, smooth, medium-bodied, subtle sweetness. Light in colour. Recommended with water, possibly as an after-dinner drink.

Kinclaith

Producing region: Lowland.
Age: distilled 1966, then distilled 1967 and variable vintage ages.
Address: Gordon and MacPhail, 58–60 South Street, Elgin. Available from U.K. spirit retailers and other specialist outlets; mainly European export markets. Also available from William Cadenhead Ltd. – see 'De luxe blends'.

Full-bodied.

Knockdhu

Producing region: Highland.
Age: distilled 1974 and variable vintage ages.
Address: Gordon and MacPhail, 58–60 South Street, Elgin. Available from U.K. spirit retailers and specialist outlets; mainly European export markets.

Lingering taste, medium-bodied.

Lagavulin
(*pronounced Lagavoolin*)

Producing region: Islay.
Age: 12 years old.
Address: Lagavulin, Port Ellen, Islay.
Parent company: Guinness plc. Available from all types of U.K. outlets. Its export markets are Europe, U.S.A., Japan, Australia, Africa, South America.

The distillery, like all those on Islay, was built on the shoreline to make possible the despatch and receipt of goods to and from small coasting vessels. Lagavulin comes from the Gaelic, meaning 'the mill in the hollow' and you can still see some ancient millstones lying on the ground near the first distillery, which was known as the Malt Mill. On one side of Lagavulin Bay is the ruined Dunyveg Castle whose name is a corruption of the Gaelic, Dun-naomhaig 'the fort of the little ships'. A seat of the MacDonalds, Lords of the Isles, in 1314 more than 1000 Islay warriors embarked at Lagavulin to fight for Robert the Bruce at Bannockburn, hence the name of the castle.

Illicit distilling had been going on at Lagavulin for some time when William Graham and his son Alexander converted the buildings into a legal distillery. In 1878 James Mackie's nephew Peter Mackie paid his first visit to Islay. He succeeded his uncle as head of Mackie and Co Ltd., and put his own stamp on the company and Lagavulin. Part of his zest for experiment included the Malt Mill distillery which he converted from older buildings in 1908 to distill whisky according to the techniques believed to have been used by the pre-industrial Islay distillers. The stills were much smaller than Lagavulin's, only peat was burned in the kiln and the final product was quite different from their previous malts. In 1962 Malt Mill distillery was closed down and its stills added to those of Lagavulin. Another link with the past was broken a few years later. Since 1924 the company-owned puffer *SS Pibroch* had been transporting barley, coal and empty casks from White Horse Distillers in

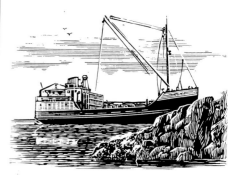

LAPHROAIG®

UNBLENDED
ISLAY MALT SCOTCH WHISKY

10 years old

The most richly flavoured of all Scotch whiskies

DISTILLED AND BOTTLED IN SCOTLAND BY

D. JOHNSTON & CO., (LAPHROAIG) LTD., LAPHROAIG DISTILLERY, ISLE OF ISLAY.

40%vol

75cl

Glasgow to Lagavulin and returning with filled casks. She was succeeded by a motor vessel in 1956 but in the 1970s it was decided to despatch whisky using the ferries. The distillery is open to the public.

Smoky, peaty, mellow, full-bodied, lingering taste. Unmistakeable, though it may not be to everyone's taste. Dark colour. Recommended with water.

Laphroaig
(pronounced Lafroig)

Producing region: Islay.
Age: 10 years old.

Address: Laphroaig Distillery, Port Ellen, Islay.
Parent company: Whitbread and Co. plc.
Available from all types of U.K. outlets, and abroad.

Laphroaig is a Gaelic word meaning 'the beautiful hollow by the broad bay'. The distillery was begun in 1815 on Islay, one of the farthest south of the Western Isles of Scotland, in a little bay sheltered by small rocky islands.

Smoky, peaty, medicinal, tangy. Quite unmistakeable. Recommended neat or with a little cool water.

Ledaig

Producing region: Highland.
Age: distilled 1972.

Address: Gordon and MacPhail, 58–60 South Street, Elgin.
Available from U.K. spirit retailers and other specialist outlets; mainly European export markets.

This is the old name given to the malt now produced as Tobermory by Tobermory Distillers Ltd. The distillery is the only one on the island of Mull.

Recommended as a pre-dinner drink.

Linkwood

Producing region: Highland.
Age: 12 years old.
Address: Linkwood Distillery, Elgin.
Parent company: Guinness plc.
Widely available.

Peter Brown, factor of the Shafield estates in Morayshire and Banffshire and a great agricultural improver, built the distillery in 1821. The premises were rebuilt by his son in the 1870s and extended in the 1890s, and production capacity doubled, with Linkwood, hitherto little known beyond the district, fetching a good price in the markets of the south. It was bought in the 1930s by Scottish Malt Distillers, part of Distillers Company Ltd., and Linkwood was in much demand from the blending companies in the DCL group. Linkwood is today a complex of modern distillery buildings and old warehouses, and even the swans on the dam serve a purpose – to keep the weeds down! The distillery is open to the public.

Refreshing, medium-bodied, subtle spirit, quite smoky. A personal favourite.

Longmorn

Producing region: Highland.
Age: 15 years old.
Address: Longmorn Distillery, Elgin.
Parent company: The Seagram Company Ltd.
Available in the U.K. in selected hotels, bars and spirit retailers; exported worldwide.

Longmorn comes from Lhanmorgund meaning 'place of the holy man'. John Duff, already an experienced distiller, chose the site three miles south of Elgin in 1894, and the distillery has enjoyed continuous production since. The distillery continues to use local spring water and peat from the nearby Mannoch Hills, and has one of the few remaining private floor maltings. The distillery combines the old and the new: it still has small wooden washbacks and an ancient steam-engine, and yet a modern waste-heat boiler. The distillery is open to the public.

Mellow, lingering taste, smooth, malty, medium-bodied. Pale amber colour.

Longrow

Producing region: Campbeltown.
Age: 12 years old.
Address: Springbank Distillery, Campbeltown, Argyll.
Parent company: J. and A. Mitchell and Co. Ltd.
Available in speciality shops in the U.K.; exported mainly to the U.S.A. and Italy.

—— Est. 1824 ——

Longrow

1973

**CAMPBELTOWN
SINGLE MALT
SCOTCH WHISKY**

Distilled and Bottled in Scotland by
J & A Mitchell & Co Ltd
75cl   SPRINGBANK DISTILLERY   46 % Vol
CAMPBELTOWN ARGYLL
SCOTLAND

PRODUCE OF SCOTLAND

ESTABLISHED 1824

The

MACALLAN

*Single Highland Malt
Scotch Whisky*

YEARS **10** OLD

DISTILLED AND BOTTLED BY
THE MACALLAN DISTILLERS LTD.
CRAIGELLACHIE · SCOTLAND

BOTTLED IN SCOTLAND

40% vol   75 cl ℮

A fascinating malt which exhibits the classic characteristics of a Campbeltown, verging on an Islay.

Smoky, peaty. Pale in colour.

The Macallan

Producing region: Highland.
Age: 7 years old – Italy only; 10 years old – mainly export and duty free; 18 and 25 years old – in all markets.
Address: Macallan Distillery, Craigellachie, Banffshire.
Available in the U.K.; exported to the U.S.A., Canada, Europe, Japan, Australia and elsewhere.

The distillery lies next to the Ringorm Burn near the River Spey – the site of whisky-making for generations. The Macallan attributes its success to the use of particularly small copper stills and the use of expensive and increasingly scarce oak casks that have contained sherry, for

maturing the whisky. The distillery is open to the public.

Sherried, mellow, full-bodied, smooth. A very stylish malt and a personal favourite.

Macduff

Producing region: Highland.
Age: distilled 1963 and following years as selected.
Address: Gordon and MacPhail, 58–60 South Street, Elgin.
Available from U.K. spirit retailers and other specialist outlets; mainly European export markets.

The distillery was built in 1962 and bought by William Lawson Distillers ten years later. Cooling water is drawn from the River Deveron and the malt is sometimes sold under the name **Glen Deveron.**

MacPhail's

Producing region: Highland.
Age: 5, 8, 10, 15, 25 years old and vintage ages.
Address: Gordon and MacPhail, 58–60 South Street, Elgin.
Available from U.K., spirit retailers and other specialist outlets; exported worldwide.

A Speyside malt which is matured in oak sherry casks.

Miltonduff

Producing region: Highland.
Age: 5 and 12 years old.
Address: Miltonduff Distillery, Elgin.
Parent company: Hiram Walker and Sons (Scotland) plc.
Available in the U.K.; its export markets are worldwide.

Miltonduff is the largest of Hiram Walker's malt distilleries, occupying part of the site of an ancient monastery near Pluscarden Priory on the great barley-growing plain between Elgin and Forres – the plain of Pluscarden or so-called 'Garden of Scotland'. According to legend, after an ancient abbot blessed the waters of the nearby Black Burn the drink distilled from them was called 'aqua vitae'. The stone on which the abbot knelt became the site of the malt mill, while the distillery's old mash house, re-built in 1824, was once the brewhouse of the monks. In 1974 the production facilities were expanded and modernized. The distillery is open to the public.

For 12 years old: *mellow, full-bodied, aromatic, lingering taste, malty. Recommended with water.*

Oban

Producing region: Highland.
Age: 12 years old.
Address: Oban Distillery, Oban.
Parent company: Guinness plc.

This malt comes in an unusual bottle with a cork closure. It is located at Oban – the 'Charing Cross of the Highlands'. The distillery is open to the public.

Medium-bodied.

Old Fettercairn

Producing region: Highland.
Age: 10 years old.
Address: Whyte and Mackay Distillers, Dalmore House, 296–8 St. Vincent Street, Glasgow.
Parent company: Lonrho plc.
Available in U.K. public houses, specialist retailers and some

supermarkets; exported to France, Italy, Portugal, Korea in particular. Also available from international duty-free shops.

The distillery was in production in the 1820s. At one point the chairman of the distillery company was Sir John Gladstone, father of the great British prime minister, W.E. Gladstone.

Peaty, full-bodied, aromatic, lingering taste, smooth. Dark golden colour. Recommended with a little water.

Old Pulteney

Producing region: Highland.
Age: 8, 15 years old, distilled 1961 and vintage years.
Address: Gordon and MacPhail, 58–60 South Street, Elgin.
Available from U.K. spirit retailers and other specialist shops; its various export markets are mainly European.

The Pulteney distillery is the most northerly on the mainland. It was established at Wick in 1826 by James Henderson who had had a small pot distillery further inland for almost 30 years. The port of Wick provided easy transport in the days before the coming of the railway, and the sea provided easy disposal of effluent. The town is divided by the Wick river and the south side is known as Pulteney Town. Pulteney was sold as a single malt throughout provincial towns in Scotland and England until quite late in the last century. The distillery was acquired by Hiram Walker in 1955 and re-equipped. Today it is available from the independent bottlers Gordon and MacPhail.

Subtle peatiness and a fine bouquet.

Port Ellen

Producing region: Islay
Age: distilled 1970 and vintage years as selected.
Address: Gordon and MacPhail, 58–60 South Street, Elgin.
Available in the U.K.; European export markets.

Not as heavy as some Islay whiskies.

Rosebank

Producing region: Lowland
Age: 8 years old.
Address: Rosebank Distillery,
Camelon, Falkirk.
Parent company: Guinness plc.

According to Alfred Barnard in *The Whisky Distilleries of the United Kingdom* (1887), the site of this distillery had been chosen 'on account of the inexhaustable supply of water'. But there were other advantages from its location – not least being sited on the banks of the Forth and Clyde Canal, placed near the main road and near a coalfield which provided cheaply transported fuel. Although not boasting the splendid isolation of many of the Highland distilleries, it was set in wooded parkland. Its history on the present site dates back to 1840 when James Rankine acquired the maltings of the Camelon Distillery on the east bank of the canal, and began distilling there. Later, through prudent management, the distillery survived the Pattison crash. In 1914 Scottish Malt Distillers, part of Distillers Company Ltd., was formed to concentrate the resources of five Lowland malt whisky distilleries, including Rosebank, at a time of deepening recession in the industry. Today, the Forth and Clyde Canal is closed to navigation and Falkirk has expanded so that Rosebank is now in an industrial area. Rosebank is one of those rare malts to be triple-distilled. The distillery is open to the public.

Dry, well-balanced, light.
Recommended as a pre-dinner drink.

Royal Lochnagar

Producing region: Highland.
Age: 'over 12 years'.
Address: Lochnagar Distillery,
Crathie, Deeside, Aberdeenshire.
Parent company: Guinness plc.
Available from U.K. spirit retailers,
supermarkets and on licensed
premises; in Germany, France, the
U.S.A., Italy, Japan, Australia and
Portugal.

In 1845 John Begg took a long lease out on 120 acres of land, part of which was the Lochnagar mountain.

DISTILLED AT ROYAL LOCHNAGAR DISTILLERY

ESTD 1845

Royal
LOCHNAGAR
YEARS 12 OLD
Single Highland Malt

SCOTCH WHISKY
PRODUCED IN SCOTLAND
AT ROYAL LOCHNAGAR DISTILLERY
JOHN BEGG LTD., GLASGOW G2 SCOTLAND

BY APPOINTMENT TO: THE LATE QUEEN VICTORIA
THE LATE KING EDWARD VII & THE LATE KING GEORGE V

Springbank

Producing region: Campbeltown
Age: 12 and 15 years old are popular. The 21 years old is to be promoted more.
Address: Springbank Distillery, Campbeltown, Argyll.
Parent company: J. and A. Mitchell and Co. Ltd.
Available in some U.K. restaurants and public houses, and from spirit retailers and selected stores; available worldwide – it claims to be the biggest-selling malt in Japan.

The distillery is one of a rare breed of distilleries still owned by descendants of the founders – in this case, the Mitchells, reputedly Scotland's oldest distilling family. The present distillery was built in 1828 on the site of the previous illicit distillery of Archibald Mitchell, the great, great grandfather of the present managing director. Springbank survived the collapse of the distilling industry in Campbeltown, and has always maintained a reputation for quality. It prides itself on not chill-filtering its products. Its 21 years old, in particular, has been acclaimed as a classic malt.

Delicate, mellow, smooth, yet full-bodied with a lingering taste. Unusually light and un-peaty for a Campbeltown. Pale, no colouring added. The 12 years old is recommended during the day, the 21 years old after dinner. A personal favourite.

ESTABLISHED 1828

SPRINGBANK
CAMPBELTOWN
SINGLE MALT

SCOTCH WHISKY
PRODUCT OF SCOTLAND
DISTILLED BY J. AND A. MITCHELL & CO. LTD.
SPRINGBANK DISTILLERY
Campbeltown · Argyll · Scotland

To the north of the mountain, an area which was popular with illicit distillers, he built a distillery. Later, the proximity of Balmoral Castle, the fairytale Deeside palace of Queen Victoria, helped to spread the fame of Royal Lochnagar whisky, and John Begg was shrewd enough to exploit the fact to publicize his drink. In 1848 he invited Queen Victoria to visit his distillery. He records in his diary that 'the Prince of Wales was going to carry his glass quickly to his mouth. I checked him saying it was very strong, and so he did not take but a very small drop. 'John Begg', at full distillery strength, may be taken only in small pegs – even by Royalty! The visit must have been a great success, for it was followed within days by the granting of a Royal Warrant of Appointment as a supplier to the Queen. John Begg saw that the future of the whisky trade lay in blends and his blended whiskies became world famous. The company came to advertise its brands under the memorable slogan: 'Take a peg of John Begg'.

The distillery is open to the public.

Sweet, full-bodied, clean taste. Pale colour. Recommended with or without water.

Sheep Dip

Producing region: Campbeltown
Age: 8 years old.
Address: M.J. Dowdeswell and Co. Ltd., Oldbury on Severn, Bristol.
Parent company: Argyll Foods.
Available in the U.K. from spirit retailers, supermarkets and large stores, and on licensed premises; exported to the U.S.A., Canada, Australia and New Zealand.

This whisky was first sold in deepest Gloucestershire where farmers refer to whisky as 'sheep dip'! The product sold well and is now more widely available.

Peaty. Pale colour. Recommended without water.

Strathisla

(pronounced Stratheyela)

Producing region: Highland
Age: 8, 15, 21 years old and others.
Address: Strathisla Distillery, Keith, Banffshire
Parent Company: The Seagram Company Ltd.
Also available from William Cadenhead Ltd.

This beautiful distillery in its picturesque setting has a claim to being one of the oldest established distilleries in the Highlands – Celtic monks are mentioned as having made heather ale there in 1208, and it is mentioned in a lease of 1785 drawn up between the Earl of Findlater and Seafield and Alexander Milne and George Taylor 'for the purposes of building a distillery'. The name of the distillery frequently changed from Milton to Strathisla, and reverted to Strathisla in May 1951 following its purchase by The Seagram Company of Canada. It is at the heart of Chivas Regal, a de luxe blend. The distillery is open to the public.

Sherried, aromatic, full-bodied, smooth. Recommended as an after-dinner drink.

Talisker

Producing region: Highland.
Age: 8 years in the U.K., 12 years elsewhere.
Address: Talisker Distillery, Carbost, Isle of Skye.
Parent company: Guinness plc.
Available in the U.K. in speciality outlets and exported worldwide.

Talisker is the only distillery on the Isle of Skye, dating from 1833. It nestles in the lee of the Cnoc nan Speireag ('Hawk Hill') and takes its water from a burn there. Although technically a Highland malt its whisky is reminiscent of its isolated seabound origins. The distillery is open to the public.

Peaty, full-bodied, aromatic. Pale in colour. Recommended with or without water or just with ice.

Tamdhu

Producing region: Highland.
Age: 10 and 15 years old.
Address: Tamdhu Distillery, Knockando, Aberlour, Banffshire.
Parent company: The Highland Distilleries Co. plc.
Available from U.K. spirit retailers and on licensed premises; it has 25 different export markets, notably France, Germany and Australia.

The distillery was built by The

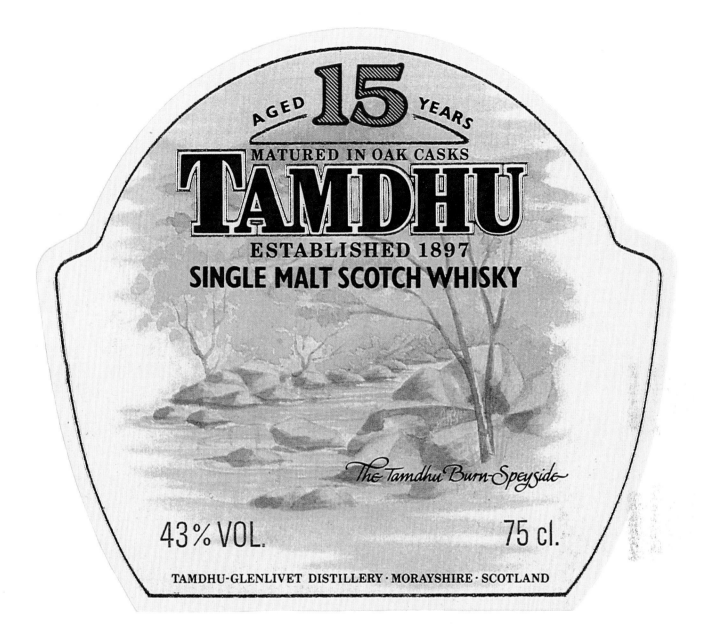

AGED **15** YEARS
MATURED IN OAK CASKS
TAMDHU
ESTABLISHED 1897
SINGLE MALT SCOTCH WHISKY

The Tamdhu Burn-Speyside

43% VOL.   75 cl.

TAMDHU-GLENLIVET DISTILLERY · MORAYSHIRE · SCOTLAND

Tamdhu-Glenlivet Distillery Company in 1896–97. After the Second World War, a new filter plant was built and the distillery plant renewed. In 1972 two new stills were added as well as a new boiler-house of considerably greater capacity. Tamdhu boasts its own maltings, and has been designed to be the group's showpiece distillery. There is a long viewing corridor to allow a sight of the still-house, receiver room, mash house and tun room. Tamdhu is on the Speyside Malt Whisky Trail, and the old Knockando Railway Station has been converted into a reception centre for visitors. The distillery is open to the public.

Delicate, sweet, mellow, medium-bodied. Recommended with water.

Tamnavulin-Glenlivet

Producing region: Highland.
Age: 10 years old.
Address: Tamnavulin-Glenlivet Distillery, Tomnavoulin, Ballindalloch, Banffshire.
Parent company: The Invergorden Distillers (Holdings) Ltd.
Available in the U.K. and exported worldwide.

The name translates from the Gaelic as 'the mill on the hill', and the River Livet flows past the distillery. Today the mill has been converted into a visitors' centre and there is a picnic area on the banks of the Livet. Tamnavulin is a light-coloured malt because, the producers maintain, no caramel colouring is added. Water from the Livet is used in the distillation processes, but the water from which the actual spirit is produced comes from a spring in the hills above the distillery.

Delicate, sweet, mellow, refreshing. Pale colour.

Tomatin
(pronounced as in 'satin')

Producing region: Highland.
Age: 5 and 10 years old.
Address: The Tomatin Distillery Company Ltd., Tomatin, Inverness-shire.
Available from U.K. supermarkets, spirit retailers, restaurants and hotels; in the U.S.A., Europe and Japan.

The company was established near the village of Tomatin near Inverness in 1897. It is a particularly romantic and historical setting. The distillery draws its water from the Alt na Frith – 'free burn' in Gaelic – from which whisky has almost certainly been distilled for centuries. Close to the distillery stands the 'Old Laird's House', parts of which date back to the 15th century. Drovers used to refresh themselves at the house's still after driving their stock through high mountain passes on their way to Tomatin's cattle pens. Nearby is the Hill of Parting – a poignant place where the Highland clans were disbanded after their bloody defeat by the English at Culloden. The distillery is very much a product of modern times, however. With the help of automation, it is Scotland's biggest-producing malt whisky distillery. Complete operation of the wash stills and the spirit stills is controlled at the push of a button. All other unattended operations within the distillery are monitored from the still-house, including the operation of three large pumps on the Findhorn, half a mile away, which provide cooling waters for the condensers of the stills. At present, the distillery produces a staggering 5 million proof gallons annually. Tomatin claims the blenders use more of their malt whisky than any other for blending. The distillery is open to the public.

Delicate, light-bodied, smooth. Dark colour. Recommended with water and as an after-dinner drink (for the 10 years old whisky).

Tomintoul
(pronounced as in 'owl')

Producing region: Highland
Address: Whyte and Mackay Distillers, Dalmore House, 296–8 St. Vincent Street, Glasgow.

Parent company: Lonrho plc. Available in the U.K. in pubs, specialist retailers and has a very limited supermarket distribution; export markets are France, Italy, Portugal, Korea; also available in duty-free shops.

The distillery is a newcomer, built a mere 20 years ago in the highest village in the Highlands. Over 52,000 litres (11,440 gals.) of alcohol are made there every week and there is warehousing for 10 million litres (2.2 million gals.).

Lingering taste, light-bodied, smooth, round. Dark golden colour. Recommended as an after-dinner drink.

Tormore

Producing region: Highland.
Age: 10 years old.
Address: Tormore Distillery, Advie, Grantown-on-Spey, Morayshire.
Parent company: Whitbread and Co. plc.

Available in all types of outlets in the U.K. and abroad.

Tormore is notable for being the first completely new malt whisky distillery to be erected in the Highlands this century. It was designed by the architect Sir Albert Richardson to 'blend' into the countryside. The distillery came on stream in 1959. The workers' houses were designed as part of the overall plan, and there is a curling pond and imitation water-mill. Above the cooperage, a chiming clock strikes up on the hour with the tune Highland Laddie. On the day that the distillery was officially opened, a 'time capsule' was deposited in its forecourt. It was made in the form of a pot still and contained a tregnum of Long John Whisky, a treatise on how Scotch is made, a history of the whisky industry, names of plant employees, an American dollar (to symbolize the importance of the U.S. market), the names of all the Scottish clans, and samples of the grain, peat, cask staves and water used in the distillery!

Smooth.

VATTED MALTS

All Malt

Age: 12 years old.
Address: Berry Bros. and Rudd Ltd., 3 St James's Street, London SW1.
Available in the U.K. from Berry Bros. and Rudd Ltd's retail shops at 3 St James's Street, London, and Houndmills, Basingstoke; exported to Belgium, The Netherlands, Spain and Switzerland.

Introduced in 1943, All Malt is a mixture of Highland malts, all at least 12 years old. It is only available in limited quantities.

Smoky, peaty, mellow, smooth, medium-bodied. Medium dark colour. Recommended as an after-dinner drink or anytime in a cold, damp climate.

Berry's Pure Malt

Age: 12 years old.
Address: Berry Bros. and Rudd Ltd., 3 St James's Street, London SW1.
Available in the U.K. from Berry Bros. and Rudd Ltd's retail shops at 3 St. James's Street, London, and Houndmills, Basingstoke; exported to France, Canada and Switzerland.

This brand is a mixture of Speyside malts all over 12 years of age.

Mellow, clean taste, malty, smooth. Medium-bodied.

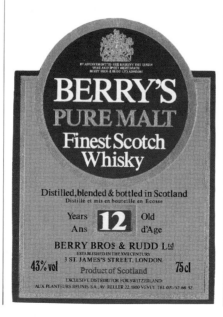

Copper Pot

Age: 8 years old.
Address: George Morton Ltd., Chapel Bond, Eastern Road, Montrose.
Parent company: Analgamated Distilled Products plc.
Available in the U.K. mainly on licenced premises; limited export markets.

A delightful name. Introduced in 1979, it is a mixture of Speyside and Islay malts.

Highland Fusilier

Age: 8 and 15 years old.

Address: Gordon and MacPhail,
58–60 South Street, Elgin.
Available from U.K. spirit retailers
and other specialist outlets; various
export markets – mainly European.

An award-winning vatted malt,
Highland Fusilier is available at high
strength and with a personalized label
for larger orders.

Lindsay

Age: 8 years old.
Address: Clydesdale Scotch Whisky
Co. Ltd., 8 Dorset Square, London
NW1.
Parent company: Clydesdale Scotch
Whisky Co. Ltd.
Available in the U.S.A.

This brand combines malts from the
Highland region, including The
Macallan and Miltonduff.

*Mellow, clean taste, smooth, full-
bodied, malty. Pale in colour.
Recommended with water.*

His Excellency Pure Malt

Age: 12 years old.
Address: Bartels, Rawlings Export
Ltd., 32–4 Borough High Street,
London SE1.
Parent company: Bartels Rawlings
International

Available in U.K. licensed
premises; in France, Spain,
Germany, Singapore, Malaysia,
Belgium, Jordan and elsewhere.

*Delicate, mellow, smooth, clean taste,
malty. Reddish colour. Recommended
without water as an after-dinner drink.*

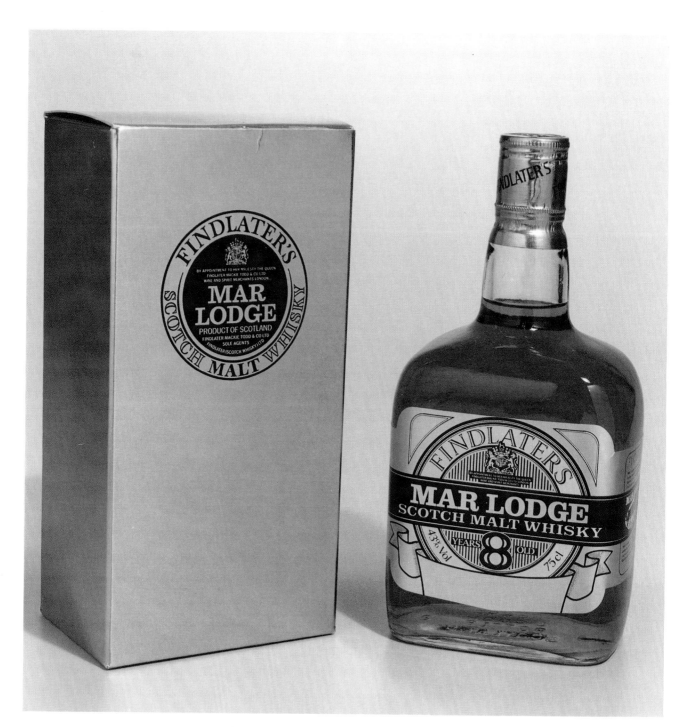

Mar Lodge

Age: 8 years old
Address: Findlater Mackie Todd and Co. Ltd., Windsor Avenue, Merton Abbey, London SW19. Limited U.K. sales but exported worldwide.

Has been available for some time. For more details, see 'Standard blends'.

Smooth, soft peat smoke flavour.

Old Elgin

Age: 8 and 15 years old, and vintage ages
Address: Gordon and MacPhail, 58–60 South Street, Elgin.
Available from U.K. spirit retailers and other specialist outlets; mainly European export markets.

This vatted malt is produced from whiskies in the district of Elgin and its environs.

120

Old Montrose

Age: 8 and 12 years old
Address: Montrose Whisky Company Ltd., 16B West Central Street, London W.C.1.

Exported worldwide.

Mellow, light-bodied, smooth, fruity. Dark in colour. Recommended without water.

Pride of Islay

Age: 12 and 20 years old
Address: Gordon and MacPhail, 58–60 South Street, Elgin. Available from U.K. spirit retailers and other specialist outlets; mainly European export markets.

Gordon and MacPhail produce four brands in this range of regional malts – see below.

Pungent and typical of Islay.

Pride of the Lowlands

Age: 12 years old.
Address: Gordon and MacPhail, 58–60 South Street, Elgin. Available from U.K. spirit retailers and other specialist shops; various export markets – mainly European.

As the name suggests, this vatted malt is from the Lowlands.

Mellow, soft.

Pride of Orkney

Age: 12 years old.
Address: Gordon and MacPhail, 58–60 South Street, Elgin. Available from U.K. spirit retailers and other specialist outlets; various export markets – mainly European.

The two most northerly distilleries in Scotland are situated on the Orkney Isles.

Peaty.

Pride of Strathspey

Age: 12, 25 years and vintage ages.
Address: Gordon and MacPhail, 58–60 South Street, Elgin. Available from U.K. spirit retailers and other specialist outlets; various export markets – mainly European.

This vatted malt contains whiskies distilled on Speyside, the famous whisky area whose commercial centre is Elgin where Gordon and MacPhail started in 1895. The label on the bottle shows Telford's single-span bridge over the River Spey at Craigellachie. Another award-winning brand from G and M.

Refreshing, dry.

The Strathconon

Age: 12 years old.
Address: James Buchanan and Co. Ltd., Buchanan House, 3 St. James's Square, London SW1.
Parent company: Guinness plc

Malty, quite heavy, Recommended as an after-dinner drink.

The Strathspey

Address: D. Cameron and Company Ltd., Rothes, Morayshire.
Parent company: International Distillers and Vintners Ltd. Available from U.K. spirit retailers and in public houses and clubs.

Mellow, full-bodied, smooth. Recommended as an after-dinner drink.

STANDARD BLENDS

Auld Sandy

Address: Balls Brothers Ltd.,
313 Cambridge Heath Road,
London E2.
Available in the U.K. from all Balls Brothers branches, specialist wine shops, wine bars.

The brand name was registered by William Austin Balls at the beginning of the 20th century. It is sold exclusively by Balls Brothers, the wine and spirit merchants.

Smoky, clean taste, smooth, medium-bodied. Medium, peaty-brown colour.

Bailie Nicol Jarvie

Address: Nicol Anderson and Co Ltd., 186 Commercial Street, Leith, Edinburgh.
Parent company: Macdonald and Muir Ltd.
Available in the U.K.

The Bailie Nicol Jarvie blend was created by Nicol Anderson in 1884. It takes its name from a colourful real-life figure in Scottish history – Bailie Nicol Jarvie. He was a Glasgow magistrate (or Bailie) shortly after the time of the Jacobite Rising of 1715. He was cousin to Rob Roy and it is the Bailie's encounters in securing a secret meeting with Rob Roy which have made him familiar to us, through the writings of Sir Walter

Scott in his novel *Rob Roy*. The blend is said to have been a firm favourite during the Boer War. The bottle and label bear the same design as the original packaging.

Delicate, smooth, medium-bodied. Reddish colour.

Ballantine's

Address: George Ballantine and Son Ltd., 3 High Street, Dumbarton.
Parent company: Hiram Walker and Sons (Scotland) plc.
Available in the U.K. and exported worldwide.

A popular brand worldwide. The company's main storage warehouses for Ballantine's at Dumbarton are guarded by a gaggle of geese known as Ballantine's Scotch Watch!

Delicate, peaty.

THE BAILIE NICOL JARVIE BLEND

→ OF ←

Old Scotch Whisky,

Sole Proprietors,

NICOL ANDERSON & Co., LTD

QUEEN'S DOCK

LEITH

PRODUCE OF SCOTLAND.

SPECIAL.

Bell's Decanter

Address: Arthur Bell and Sons plc, Cherrybank, Perth.
Parent company: Guinness plc. Widely available throughout the world.

This blend of whiskies is bottled in a distinctive bell-shaped decanter made of porcelain. It started life in the 1920s as a traditional decanter shape made of blue glass. Then in the 1930s it became a blue porcelain bell shape. In the 1950s Royal Doulton began producing the more familiar brown and gold decanter. In 1960 production was taken over by Spode and in 1965 by Wade. Limited edition commemorative decanters were produced for the marriage of Prince Charles and Lady Diana, and the birth of Prince William.

Recommended with or without water.

Bell's Extra Special

Address: Arthur Bell and Sons plc, Cherrybank, Perth.
Parent company: Guinness plc. Widely available in the U.K. and abroad.

Bell's Extra Special is one of the biggest-selling brands in the U.K. It is a blend of about 30 different whiskies. The company was founded at Perth in 1825 and expanded when the demand for blended whiskies grew. The need for adequate reserves of malt whisky became imperative and in the 1930s the firm bought the Blair Athol, Inchgower and Dufftown-Glenlivet distilleries. In 1973 the company built the Pittyvaich-Glenlivet distillery about 400 metres from Dufftown-Glenlivet, which produces an 8-year old malt for blending purposes. In 1983 the Bladnoch distillery at Wigtown, which prod-

uces a Lowland malt, was bought. Bell's has all its production and administration facilities in Scotland.

Well-rounded, lingering taste, hint of smoke. Pale colour. Recommended with or without water.

Beneagles

Address: Waverley Vintners, P.O. Box 22, Crieff Road, Perth.
Parent company: Scottish and Newcastle Breweries plc. Available on licensed premises in the U.K.

The Beneagles name is reputedly inspired by the construction of the famous Gleneagles golfing hotel. It is the standard house brand of Waverley Vintners, the wholesale wine and spirit merchants.

Sherried, mellow, clean taste, medium-bodied. Rich golden colour.

Benmore Selected

Address: Benmore Distilleries Ltd., Trafalgar House, 75 Hope Street, Glasgow.
Parent company: Guinness plc.
Available in France, Belgium, Italy and the Canary Islands.

Benmore Distilleries Ltd. was founded in 1920 to supply malt whiskies for blending. Benmore comes from the Gaelic for high mountain and from this were derived the slogans 'The Peak of Scotch' and 'The Pinnacle of Perfection' to describe the company's products. The company acquired four distilleries, including the Dallas Dhu distillery near Forres (see 'Single malts').

Soon after its formation, the company expanded its activities by producing its own blends in bulk. In 1923 the first brand name to be registered as a blended Scotch was Dallas Mhor. The venture into blending proved so successful that by 1929 it was the supply of blended whiskies which had become Benmore's main concern. In that year, too, the company began producing Dallas Mhor in bottles, albeit in a small way. The demand for the bottled product proved so encouraging that within two years the company began bottling its Benmore blends.

The company decided to offer their bottled blends for sale to export markets and by the mid-1930s concentrated on selling their most popular brand, Benmore Liqueur Scotch Whisky. Because of the possible confusion over the word 'liqueur', which to the public meant a sweetened spirit, the brand name was altered first to Benmore Blended Scotch Whisky and later, to Benmore Selected Scotch Whisky – the name by which it is known today.

Delicate, mellow, clean taste, smooth. Dark in colour. Recommended with or without water, and with mixers.

Benmore Special Reserve

Address: Benmore Distilleries Ltd., Trafalgar House, 75 Hope Street, Glasgow.
Parent company: Guinness plc.
Available in France, Belgium, Italy and the Canary Islands.

See Benmore Selected, above, for historical note.

Delicate, mellow, medium-bodied. Dark in colour. Recommended with or without water, and with mixers.

Black and White

Address: James Buchanan and Co Ltd., Buchanan House, 3 St. James's Square, London SW1.
Parent company: Guinness plc

This well-known blend was created by James Buchanan. For a time it was known as House of Commons, but people would ask for the whisky in the black bottle with the white label – hence the name.

Light-bodied, tangy.

Black Barrel

Address: H. Stenham Ltd., 43 Lodge Avenue, Elstree, Hertfordshire.
Exported to Europe, Australia and Japan.

Henry Stenham founded this firm in 1953 and still runs it personally.

Mellow, light-bodied, smooth. Pale in colour. Recommended without water.

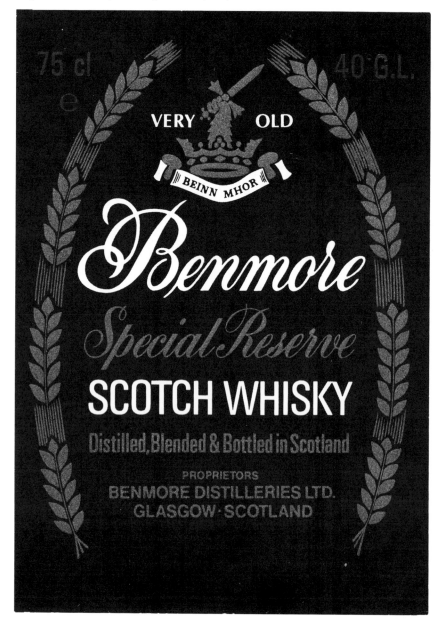

75 cl e   VERY OLD   40° G.L.

BEINN MHOR

Benmore
Special Reserve
SCOTCH WHISKY
Distilled, Blended & Bottled in Scotland
PROPRIETORS
BENMORE DISTILLERIES LTD.
GLASGOW · SCOTLAND

bottle shape and distinctive slanted label have changed little in 100 years.

Subtle, aromatic, smooth.

'BL' Gold Label

Address: Bulloch Lade and Co. Ltd., Trafalgar House, 75 Hope Street, Glasgow.
Parent company: Guinness plc. Available from U.K. spirit retailers and on licensed premises; in the U.S.A., Canada, France, Italy, Spain, Australia, New Zealand and Venezuela.

Bulloch Lade and Co., was established in 1856 by the merger of Bulloch and Co. with Lade and Co., two family-run distillers who believed their union would lead to a more prosperous future. Their optimism was soon justified. At the time of the merger, Bulloch Lade owned two distilleries, Loch Katrine and Lossit, but a year later, they were able to acquire Caol Ila Distillery on the island of Islay, off the west coast of Scotland. Caol Ila malt whisky (see 'Single malts') is still a greatly valued constituent of many blends and is an essential ingredient of 'BL' Gold Label.

Delicate, mellow, refreshing, smooth. Reddish in colour. Recommended with or without water, and with mixers.

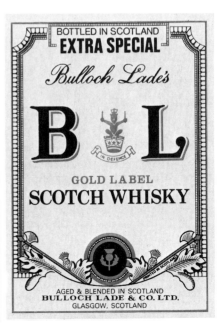

Black Bottle

Address: Gordon Graham and Co., Westthorn, 1780 London Road, Glasgow.
Parent company: Whitbread and Co. plc.
Available in all U.K. outlets.

Black Bottle was first produced by Gordon Graham and Co., a tea importers and blenders in Aberdeen since 1879, for consumption by the partners, their friends and business acquaintances. The brand's reputation spread throughout Aberdeen and the surrounding area where it was favoured by members of the local fishing community who carried the product further afield. The tea business disappeared and the partners devoted themselves to Black Bottle. The brand is advertised with the slogan 'Unspoilt by progress.' The

Catto's Rare Old Scottish Highland

Address: James Catto and Co. Ltd., Renfrew.
Parent company: International Distillers and Vintners Ltd.
Available in U.K. public houses, restaurants and from spirit retailers; widely exported but especially in the U.S.A., Canada, France, Spain and Japan.

James Catto set up in Aberdeen as a blender in 1861, selling to Scotsmen and exporting his Scotch whisky to their communities all over the world. He had an influential circle of friends in Aberdeen, particularly in the shipping world, and Catto's quickly became a leading brand with many of the big shipping companies. Sadly, James' son, Robert, was killed during the First World War and family involvement in the business came to an end. The famous wine and spirit merchants W. and A. Gilbey Ltd., eventually became the owners.

Mellow, full-bodied, smooth.

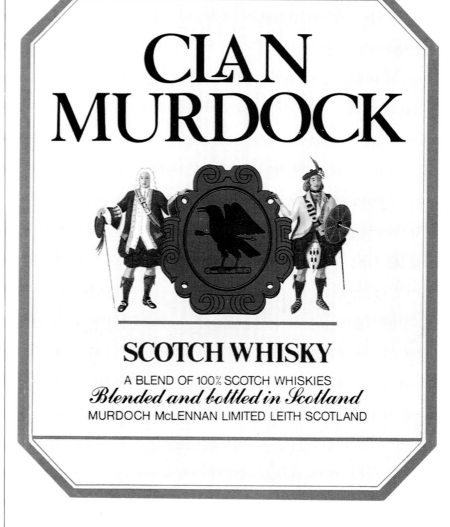

Clan Murdock

Address: Murdoch McLennan Ltd., 186 Commercial Street, Leith, Edinburgh.
Parent company: Macdonald and Muir Ltd.
Exported to South America and South Africa.

Mellow, smooth, medium-bodied. Reddish colour.

Cluny

Address: John E. McPherson and Sons Ltd., 9/21 Salamander Place, Leith, Edinburgh.
Parent company: The Invergordon Distillers Holdings Ltd.
Mainly exported, particularly the U.S.A., Canada and Italy.

Cluny is the title carried by the Chiefs of the Clan MacPherson. It is with permission of the clan that the McPherson company bottle this brand.

Cutty Sark Scots Whisky

Address: Berry Bros. and Rudd Ltd., 3 St James' Street, London SW1.
Available from U.K. spirit retailers and specialist shops. It is among the U.S.A.'s best selling 'Scots' whiskies. Also available in 130 export markets worldwide.

Cutty Sark Scots Whisky was born on 23 March 1923 in 'The Parlour' of Berry Bros. and Rudd in the heart of St. James', where a grocers shop had been doing business since 1699. The firm had sold a little of their own brands of Scotch to private customers in the U.S.A. before the First World War. There were signs that the disastrous experiment of Prohibition would not last forever, and the company now sought a new and different blend for the export trade, particularly America.

Francis Berry decided on a blend of Scotch whiskies free from caramel colouring. (Later, when asked why Cutty Sark was so pale, Hugh Rudd replied: 'Why are other whiskies so dark?') Seated round the table that day were Francis and Walter Berry, Hugh Rudd and their friend, the Scottish artist James McBey. The new whisky would need an exciting name and an eye-catching symbol. It was McBey, a keen sailor, who suggested 'Cutty Sark'.

The famous clipper had been in the news as she had just returned to England. McBey also designed the label, which remains today almost exactly as he originally drew it – right down to the hand-drawn lettering and the use of the descriptive word 'Scots' rather than the Sassenach's 'Scotch'! The colour of the label is different from his original design. McBey wanted cream to imply age. The printers accidentally produced bright yellow. And the partners decided to keep it.

When Prohibition ended in 1933, Cutty Sark was already well known and respected in America. During the Second World War, Berry Bros. kept their limited production for their customers, including G.I.s stationed in London who would queue up outside the shop to buy their ration. The brand became an important dollar-earner.

Delicate, refreshing, clean taste, smooth, malty. Pale colour.

Dewar's White Label

Address: John Dewar and Sons Ltd., Inveralmond, Perth.
Parent company: Guinness plc.
Available in the U.K., mostly from spirit retailers; exported worldwide, mainly to the U.S.A.

The company was founded in 1846 and by the turn of the century, Dewar's had become a major export brand. A big, big seller in the U.S.A. today. The company is holder of the Royal Warrant and has won six Queen's Awards for export achievement.

Clean taste, smooth, medium-bodied. Medium brown colour.

Director's Special

Address: H. Stenham Ltd., 43 Lodge Avenue, Elstree, Hertfordshire.
Available in Europe, Australia and Japan.

This family firm is, to my knowledge, still run by the man who founded it in 1953, Henry Stenham.

Mellow, light-bodied, smooth. Pale colour. Recommended without water.

The Famous Grouse

Address: Matthew Gloag and Son Ltd., Bordeaux House, Kinnoull Street, Perth.
Parent company: The Highland Distilleries Co. plc.
Among Britain's best-selling blends, available in all types of outlets; it has 80 world export markets.

In 1800 Matthew Gloag opened a grocery and wine merchants business in Perth and started dealing in whiskies by buying individual products of various pot-stills from the surrounding district. Sales were made from the shop in earthenware jars or crocks. In 1876 his son Matthew eventually took over the business and *his* daughter designed the grouse motif which a year later, began to be used as a symbol for Gloag. The whisky was originally called 'The Grouse Brand' but as it grew in popularity, it began to be referred to as 'The Famous Grouse'.

Sweet, mellow, aromatic, clean taste, smooth. Golden brown colour. Recommended with water.

Findlater's Finest

Address: Findlater Mackie Todd and Co. Ltd., Windsor Avenue, Merton Abbey, London S.W.19. Available in the U.K. from specialist outlets; exported to Spain, Italy, Holland, Japan, South America and elsewhere.

Alexander Findlater went into business at the age of 26 as a wine and spirit merchant in Dublin in 1823. Later he entered into a variety of partnerships in different English cities. In 1850 he went to London and thirteen years later Findlater Mackie Todd and Co. was started up, and soon became established as wine and spirit merchants and proprietors of Findlater's Scotch whisky.

Mellow, aromatic. Dark colour.

Glen Calder

Address: Gordon and MacPhail, 58–60 South Street, Elgin. Available from U.K. spirit retailers and other specialist outlets; various export markets – mainly European.

An award-winning blend from the independent bottlers Gordon and MacPhail. The company was established in 1895 in Elgin. This small, attractive 'city' is the traditional centre for the Speyside distilling area. The business was originally a wholesale/retail warehouse but one of the partners, James Gordon, had already been active as a whisky broker. The whisky side of the business grew and today the company not only blends its own brands but supplies blends and vatted malts exclusively to hotels and clubs. It also provides personalized labels for trade or private use, and stocks a vast range of malt whiskies. Their June 1986 wholesale list, for example, included a 1936 distilla-

tion Glen Grant, a 1939 distillation Linkwood and a 1948 distillation Strathisla!

Malty, clean taste, touch of smoke.

Glendrostan

Address: Longman Distillers Ltd., 9/21 Salamander Place, Leith, Edinburgh.
Parent company: The Invergorden Distillers Holdings Ltd.
Export worldwide.

Sweet, full-bodied, lingering taste. Medium golden colour. Reddish colour.

Glen Niven

Address: Douglas MacNiven, 186 Commercial Street, Leith, Edinburgh.
Parent company: Macdonald and Muir Ltd.
Export markets include Greece, Jordan, South Africa, Canary Islands and elsewhere.

Mellow, smooth, medium-bodied.

Gold Label

Address: Clydesdale Scotch Whisky Co. Ltd., 8 Dorset Square, London N.W.1.
Available in the U.S.A. and South America.

Mellow, full-bodied, clean taste, smooth, malty. Pale colour. Recommended with water.

Haig

Address: John Haig and Company Ltd., Haig House, Albany Street, Edinburgh.
Parent company: Guinness plc.
Widely available.

Light and smooth.

Highland Queen

Address: Macdonald and Muir Ltd., 186 Commercial Street, Leith, Edinburgh.

Parent company: Macdonald Martin Distilleries plc
Available in the U.K. mostly on licensed premises and from some specialist retailers; widely exported.

Highland Queen is the flag-carrier for Macdonald and Muir Ltd. The brand name derives from the romantic association of Leith and the original site beside the old harbour occupied by Macdonald and Muir in 1893, and the triumphal arrival of Mary Stuart at this spot in 1561. She was later to be crowned Queen of Scots, thus creating one of Scotland's most famous and loved legends. Highland Queen comes in standard and 'de luxe' blends. Malt whiskies of up to 10 years of age are used in the standard blend and the company guarantees that the blend is over five years old. The company's two malts – Glenmorangie and Glen Moray – contribute to its balance.

The company itself was founded in Leith by Roderick Macdonald and Alexander Muir in 1893. It is one of the few remaining independent family-owned and controlled companies of Scotch whisky distillers and blenders. The firm acquired the Glenmorangie Distillery, Ross-shire,

after they had started using its malt in their Highland Queen blend in the 1890s. Soon afterwards, they bought the Glen Moray-Glenlivet Distillery near Elgin. The company benefited from the Scotch whisky boom at the turn of the last century and throughout the 1930s and 1940s international popularity grew so that today Macdonald and Muir whiskies are sold in 108 world markets. The company prides itself on a tradition of high standards. In the words of the managing-director David Macdonald: 'It is no accident that the motto of our home town of Leith is "Persevere".'

Sweet, delicate, smooth, medium-bodied, mellow. Pale colour.

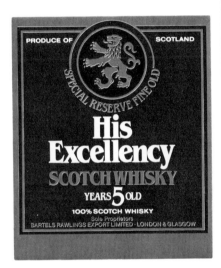

His Excellency

Address: Bartels, Rawlings Export Ltd., 32–4 Borough High Street, London S.E.1.
Parent company: Bartels Rawlings International.
Available in bottles and flagons from supermarkets, spirit retailers, public houses and hotels in the U.K.; in France, Spain, Singapore, Malta, Jordan, Australia, Belgium and South Africa.

Aromatic, clean taste, smooth, malty, medium-bodied. Reddish colour. Recommended without water as a pre-dinner drink.

J & B Rare

Address: Justerini and Brooks Ltd.,

61 St James's Street, London S.W.1.
Parent company: International Distillers and Vintners Ltd.
Available widely in the U.K. and abroad.

Light. Recommended as a daytime drink.

John Begg Blue Cap

Address: John Begg Ltd., Trafalgar House, 75 Hope Street, Glasgow.
Parent company: Guinness plc.
Available from U.K. spirit retailers and on licensed premises; in the U.S.A., Canada, Belgium, France, Germany, Madiera, Portugal and Japan.

John Begg Blue Cap is an old, established brand. John Begg acquired a

lease of part of the Lochnagar mountain near Balmoral Castle on Deeside in 1845, from where he produced Royal Lochnagar single malt whisky (see 'Single malts'). He saw that the future of the whisky industry lay with the blends. He acquired bonded warehouses, bottling and duty-paid cellars and offices in Aberdeen. The outcome was a big increase in Begg's business at home and abroad. In 1916 the company was absorbed into the Distillers Company.

Delicate, sweet, mellow, clean taste, smooth. Dark in colour. Recommended with or without water, or with mixers.

Johnnie Walker Red Label

Address: John Walker and Sons Ltd., 63 St James's Street, London S.W.1.

Parent company: Guinness plc
Available in all types of U.K. outlets; its export markets are worldwide.

Johnnie Walker Red Label is the world's largest selling Scotch whisky. It is a blend of around forty single malt and grain whiskies including Cardhu Highland malt (the Cardhu distillery was acquired by John Walker and Sons in 1893). The famous square bottle has a red and gold slanting label bearing the striding figure of John Walker, the company's founder.

John Walker purchased a grocery, wine and spirit business in Kilmarnock in 1820 and as the industrial revolution progressed and Kilmarnock grew, so did the market for his Walker's Kilmarnock Whisky. The main railway line from Glasgow via Kilmarnock to the south was completed in 1834 and travelling businessmen introduced his whisky further afield, often wrapped in

sample rolls of carpet for which the town was famous.

Overseas markets in the 19th century were reached through the 'merchant venturer' system whereby goods were entrusted to the captain of the ship who would sell them on commission at the best price he could get. Alexander Walker, John Walker's son, was an enthusiastic supporter of the system and the origins of the company's vast overseas sales (it exports over 95 per cent of its production) can be attributed to him. In 1880 a London office was opened, in 1890 and office in Sydney, Australia, an in 1897 agents were appointed in South Africa and an office opened in Birmingham.

It was at the beginning of the twentieth century that Tom Browne designed the striding Johnnie Walker figure, Lord Stevenson coined the phrase 'Johnnie Walker, born 1820–still going strong' and the name 'Walker's Kilmarnock Whisky' dropped in favour of the red and black slanted labels. Today, each of the 200 or so markets for Johnnie Walker Red Label has its own labelling requirements and over 1000 different labels are produced to meet them.

Full-bodied, refreshing. Reddish in colour. Recommended with a wide range of mixers.

Langs Supreme

Address: Lang Brothers Ltd., 100 West Nile Street, Glasgow.

Parent company: Robertson and Baxter Ltd.
Available from U.K. spirit retailers and on licensed premises; widely exported, particularly to France,

Italy, Spain, Japan and South America.

The name of Lang first became associated with wines and spirits in the 1850s when Hugh Lang kept an inn in the then rapidly expanding port of Galsgow. His three sons saw wider commercial possibilities opening up as Glasgow and the Clyde area developed as an industrial and commercial centre. In 1861 they founded Lang Brothers Limited as wine and spirit merchants. Fifteen years later, they bought the Glengoyne Distillery in Stirlingshire. From this base Lang's developed an international business with their blends of Scotch whisky. Lang's remained a family-controlled business until its acquisition in 1965 by Robertson and Baxter ltd. Glengoyne single malt whisky is at the heart of the Lang's blends.

Mellow, full-bodied, smooth. Dark colour.

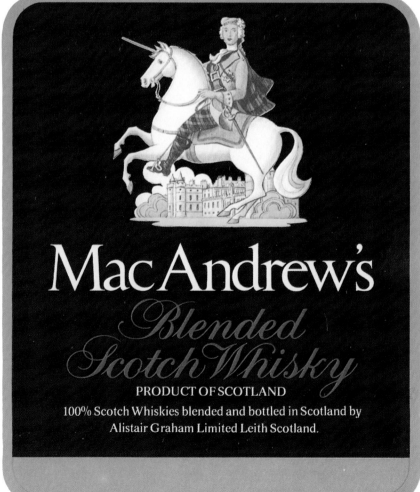

Long John

Address: Long John Distilleries, Westthorn, 1780 London Road, Glasgow.
Parent company: Whitbread and Co. plc.
Available in all types of U.K. outlets; exported to 135 countries, especially France, Germany, Sweden, Norway, Denmark, Italy and Spain.

This blend is named after Long John Macdonald who, in 1825, built a distillery at Fort William called the Ben Nevis Distillery. His original whisky was called Long John's Dew of Ben Nevis. In his book *A summer in Skye* (1864), Alexander Smith wrote of his meeting with Long John: 'This gentleman was the tallest man I ever beheld, and must in his youth been of incomparable physique.'

Queen Victoria visited Long John in his distillery in 1848 and the *Illustrated London News* recorded that he presented her with a cask of whisky. She ordered it to be kept back until the Prince of Wales attained his majority (some 15 years later).

Mellow, full-bodied, smooth. Dark colour.

MacAndrew's

Address: Alistair Graham Ltd., 186 Commercial Street, Leith, Edinburth.
Parent company: Macdonald and Muir Ltd.
Exported to South America.

MacAndrew's is named after Lord Douglas MacAndrew, a famous Scottish gentleman of the 19th century. The 'Laird' was a colourful character, renowned for his fine horsemanship and love of farming, which were practised on his estate near Inverness. The bottle label features the 'Laird' on horseback in front of his stately home. He tried to improve the standard of whisky be experimenting with new agricultural methods to produce a better quality yield of grain for whisky production.

Aromatic, smooth, medium-bodied. Reddish colour.

Major Gunn's

Address: 186 Commercial Street, Leith, Edinburgh.
Parent company: Macdonald and Muir Ltd.
Exported to South America.

Named after a well-known soldier in Scottish history, Major Gunn was a descendant of the Chief of the Clan Gunn who were based in Caithness from the 12th to the 15th centuries.

Refreshing, smooth, medium-bodied. Reddish colour.

Morton's Blended

Address: George Morton Ltd., Chapel Bond, Eastern Road, Montrose.
Parent company: Amalgamated Distilled Products plc.
Available in U.K. licensed premises and supermarkets.

The company has blended and bottled whisky for well over a century.

Mellow, full-bodied, clean taste, smooth. Dark colour.

Muirhead's

Address: Charles Muirhead and Son Ltd., 186 Commercial Street, Leith, Edinburgh.
Parent company: Macdonald and Muir Ltd.
Available in the U.K., South America and India.

The company was established in Edinburgh in 1824 as a wine merchants. Acquiring another wine-shipping company a century later, the company branched out into Scotch whisky blending, bottling and exporting.

Clean taste, smooth, medium-bodied.

Oakfield

Address: Oakfield Ltd., 100 Wellington Street, Glasgow.
Parent company: Oakfield Ltd.
Available in Scandinavia.

The man behind Oakfield is Nils Ekjord whose surname is 'Oakfield' in English. The oak tree label was designed by the owner's mother. The first bottle of Oakfield whisky was produced as late as 1976, so it is still in the process of establishing markets. The blend contains whiskies from Speyside, the Islands and elsewhere.

Delicate, mellow, light-bodied, smooth. Pale colour. Recommended with or without water.

100 Pipers

Address: Chivas Brothers, 111/113 Renfrew Road, Paisley.
Parent company: The Seagram Company Ltd.
Available in the U.K., Europe and U.S.A.

Considered a standard blend by the producers; the malt whisky produced

by Glen Keith distillery is an important constituent of this blend.

Light, fruity.

The Original Mackinlay

Address: Charles Mackinlay and Co. Ltd., 9/21 Salamander Place, Leith, Edinburgh.
Parent company: The Invergordon Distillers Holdings Ltd.
Available from U.K. spirit retailers and on licensed premises; exported worldwide.

The original Charles Mackinlay set up business in Leith in 1815. It is said that young Mr Charles used to enjoy a round of golf on the nearby course at Leith, and it was to match this sporting spirit that he conceived The Original Mackinlay. The company prospered during the 19th century and in 1907, Sir Ernest Shackleton, the explorer, asked the company to supply the official Scotch for his South Pole expedition. Empty bottles of The Original Mackinlay were discovered by a later expedition still standing on Shackleton's base-camp desk. Today a fifth-generation Mackinlay, Donald, is responsible for the blending of The Original Mackinlay since its re-introduction in 1985.

Sweet, mellow, full-bodied, lingering taste, malty. Rich amber colour.

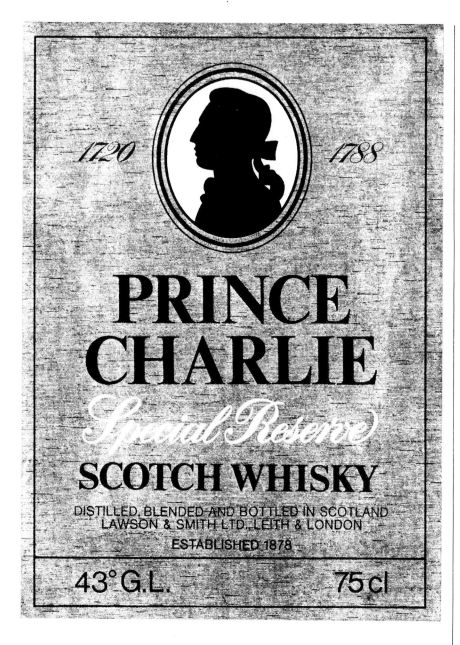

1720   1788

PRINCE CHARLIE

Special Reserve

SCOTCH WHISKY

DISTILLED, BLENDED AND BOTTLED IN SCOTLAND
LAWSON & SMITH LTD., LEITH & LONDON

ESTABLISHED 1878

43° G.L.   75cl

Queen Anne

Address: Hill, Thomson and Co. Ltd., 45 Frederick Street, Edinburgh.
Parent company: The Seagram Company Ltd.
Available in all types of U.K. outlets; exported worldwide.

Around the time of the building of Edinburgh's Georgian New Town, seeing the influx of new money into the city, William Hill started a fine wines and spirits business in 1793. His business expanded rapidly and in 1799, he moved to new larger premises in Frederick Street which has remained the head office of the company to this day. In 1857 William Thomson was taken into partnership and the company assumed its present name.

In 1880, a young man of great foresight and ability, William Shaw, joined the firm and was instrumental in building up export sales of the company's blended whiskies, Queen Anne and Something Special. His son followed him into business and the family has been continuously represented since that time.

In 1970 Hill, Thomson and Co. Ltd. merged with The Glenlivet and Glen Grant Distilleries Ltd. and The Longmorn Distilleries Ltd. The new company adopted the name The Glenlivet Distillers Ltd. and in 1978 this company was itself acquired by The Seagram Company Ltd. of Canada.

Mellow, clean taste, smooth, malty, medium-bodied. Amber colour.

Pig's Nose

Address: M.J. Dowdeswell and Co. Ltd., Oldbury-on-Severn, Bristol.
Parent company: Argyll Foods.
Available in the U.K. from spirit retailers, supermarkets and large stores, and on licensed premises; exported to the U.S.A. and New Zealand.

Among the most memorable names of Scotch whisky! Pig's Nose is four years old. It is designed to be sold alongside Sheep Dip malt whisky (see 'Single malts').

Smooth, mellow. Pale colour. Recommended with water.

Prince Charlie

Address: Lawson and Smith Ltd., 45 Frederick Street, Edinburgh.
Parent company: The Seagram Company Ltd.
Available in U.K. supermarkets and from spirit retailers; exported worldwide.

Not named after our existing Prince of Wales! In fact, this blend is a very old brand that was first registered in 1896. Lawson and Smith Ltd. was taken over by Hill, Thomson and Co. Ltd. in the 1930s.

Delicate, mellow, light-bodied, clean taste, smooth. Amber colour.

Red Hackle

Address: Lang Brothers Ltd., 100 West Nile Street, Glasgow.
Parent company: Robertson and Baxter Ltd.
Available in the U.K., France, Germany, Denmark and Japan.

The Red Hackle label is said to show the head-dress of the famous Black Watch Regiment, including a plume of red feathers in honour of their valour in 1795 at the battle of Gildermalsen. The original Hepburn and Ross partners who produced the blend, served with the regiment. Hepburn and Ross Ltd. were acquired in 1959 by Robertson and Baxter Ltd. Lang's also produce Red Hackle Reserve (see next page).

Delicate, mellow, light-bodied, clean taste, smooth (for Red Hackle 43 per cent). Dark colour.

Red Hackle Reserve

Address: Lang Brothers Ltd., 100 West Nile Street, Glasgow.
Parent company: Robertson and Baxter Ltd.
Exported widely, particularly to France, Denmark and Japan.

The producers consider this a standard blend, though at 12 years old, it has been aged for an unusually long time for this type of product.

Sherried, sweet, mellow, smooth, medium-bodied. Dark colour.

Regal Scot

Address: Clydesdale Scotch Whisky Co. Ltd., 8 Dorset Square, London N.W.1.
Available in Europe and South America.

Mellow, full-bodied, clean taste, smooth, malty. Pale in colour. Recommended with water.

St. Leger

Address: Hill, Thomson and Co. Ltd., 45 Frederick Street, Edinburgh.

Parent company: The Seagram Company Ltd.
Available in Canada and elsewhere.

The interest shown in 'light' Scotch in North America, which emerged in the late 1930s, led this introduction. The brand is named after the English horse race the St. Leger and appropriately the word approximates to the French word for 'light'. Particularly successful in the French Canadian province of Quebec.

Delicate, mellow, light-bodied, dry. Pale in colour.

Scots Grey

Address: Grey Rodgers and Co. Ltd., 9/21 Salamander Place, Leith, Edinburgh.
Parent company: The Invergordon Distillers (Holdings) Ltd.
Exported worldwide.

Despite the words 'De luxe' on the label, the producers consider this drink a standard blend.

Sweet, mellow, refreshing, smooth.

Scottish Dance

Address: H. Stenham Ltd., 43 Lodge Avenue, Elstree, Hertfordshire.
Available in Europe, Australia and Japan.

H. Stenham Ltd. was founded in 1953 and, as far as I am aware, is still run as a family business.

Mellow, light-bodied, smooth. Pale in colour. Recommended without water.

Spey Royal

Address: Glen Spey Ltd., Glen Spey Distillery, Rothes, Morayshire.
Parent company: International Distillers and Vintners Ltd.
Available from U.K. spirit retailers, public houses, and clubs; widely exported, including to the U.S.A.

Spey Royal takes its name from the famous River Spey and from the Glen Spey Distillery which the brothers Walter and Alfred Gilbey bought in 1887. Spey Royal became the company's principal brand of Scotch. Glen Spey's malt whisky forms the heart of the blend. Shortly after the purchase of Glen Spey, Queen Victoria granted the company her Royal Warrant as suppliers of wines and spirits to the Royal Household. A year later, Walter Gilbey was made a Baronet.

Mellow, smooth, medium-bodied.

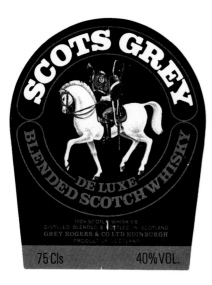

Teacher's Highland Cream

Address: Wm. Teacher and Sons Ltd., St Enoch Square, Glasgow.
Parent company: Allied Lyons. Available widely in the U.K. and abroad.

A big-selling brand in the U.K. The brand is noted for its high malt content for a standard blend.

Malty, clean tasting. Quite dark in colour. Recommended with a little water.

Usher's Green Stripe

Address: J. and G. Stewart, 21 Manor Place, Edinburgh.
Parent company: Guinness plc. Mainly intended for export to the U.S.A.

For details see below.

Usher's Old Vatted Scotch

Address: J. and G. Stewart, 21 Manor Place, Edinburgh.
Parent company: Guinness plc. Mainly intended for export to the U.S.A.

Andrew Usher was the exclusive agent for The Glenlivet from 1840, but he is best remembered for his pioneering work with blending. In 1853 he introduced vatting of different Glenlivet whiskies and then went on to blend pot still malt whisky with grain whisky.

White Horse

Address: White Horse Distillers Ltd., 99 Borron Street, Port Dundas, Glasgow.
Parent Company: Guinness plc. Available in all types of U.K. outlets. Its export markets are Europe, U.S.A., Japan, Australia, Africa and S. America.

The present day firm was founded by James Logan Mackie in 1883 in Glasgow but it would seem that the family were also in possession of the famous White Horse Inn in Canongate, Edinburgh. White Horse Close, which housed the inn, was named after the white palfrey that carried Mary Queen of Scots to and from the nearby Palace of Holyroodhouse.

The name White Horse was not officially registered until 1891. By this time James Mackie's nephew Peter Mackie had succeeded him. He had trained at the Lagavulin distillery on Islay which had been run by a partnership of James Logan Mackie and Captain Graham since 1883. It was Peter Mackie who was first to recognize the importance of a standard of whisky and a brand name for it. Hence White Horse.

'Restless Peter' built the firm up so that White Horse Distillers Ltd. was one of what was known as the 'Big Five' in the Scotch whisky world. He was a great fighter for the cause of maturing whiskies. It was also White Horse that were the pioneers with screw caps: until then bottles had been corked. In 1915 Peter Mackie bought the Craigellachie distillery on

Speyside, whose product is part of the White Horse recipe. In 1924 when Peter Mackie died, Mackie and Co. as it had been known since 1890, took its present title of White Horse Distillers Ltd., and in 1927 became part of The Distillers Company Ltd. Today White Horse products are exported to almost 200 countries.

Mellow, full-bodied, clean taste. Dark colour.

Whyte and Mackay Special

Address: Whyte and Mackay Distillers, Dalmore House, 296-8 St. Vincent Street, Glasgow.
Parent company: Lonrho plc.
Widely available in the U.K. Exported to over 80 countries.

The company goes back to 1844 when it was first established under the name of Allan and Poynter. In 1882 James Whyte, who managed the firm,

went into partnership with Charles Mackay. Their success was based on their 'Special' brand – a blend of 35 Highland malt whiskies married with a selection of grain whiskies. Whyte and Mackay became increasingly popular throughout the world, the principal markets being the U.S.A., Canada, South Africa and New Zealand. After the Second World War, there was a shortage of mature stocks and the company spent the next four years building up stocks to enable further expansion. The next move was into distilling. In 1960 they merged with the Dalmore distillery and in 1972 they acquired the Fettercairn distillery and the Tomintoul-Glenlivet distillery. In 1979 the company merged with Lonrho, the mining, textiles, hotels, newspaper and printing group. With the Guinness takeover of Distillers Company Ltd. in 1986, the company acquired several DCL brands plus U.K. domestic rights to others.

Mellow, lingering taste, clean taste, smooth, malty and round. Dark golden colour.

DE LUXE BLENDS

Avonside
Age: 8 years old.
Address: Gordon and MacPhail, 58-60 South Street, Elgin.
Available in the U.K. from spirit retailers and other specialist outlets; mainly European export markets.

This blend is prepared by Gordon and MacPhail and has been sold for over 50 years.

Fruity.

Bell's 12 Year Old De Luxe
Age: 12 years old.
Address: Arthur Bell and Sons plc, Cherrybank, Perth.
Parent Company: Guinness plc.
Available in all types of U.K. outlets and exported to all world markets.

For details, see 'Standard blends'.

Berry's Best
Age: 8 years old.
Address: Berry Bros. and Rudd Ltd., 3 St. James's Street London S.W.1.
Available from Berry Bros. and Rudd Ltd., 3 St. James's Street, London and Houndmills, Basingstoke.

No. 3 St. James's has been occupied by a single family or its associates since the 1690's when the Widow Bourne moved into the house, where she is known to have set up a grocer's shop. Her daughter married one William Pickering. By the 1750s Pickering's had become acknowledged as the best and most comprehensive of London's grocers, having as their customers the inhabitants of St. James's Palace and the Beau Monde, as epitomized by George 'Beau' Brummell, who was weighed on Berry's great scales.

It was through William Pickering that the Berry family came into the business; the first, George Berry, beginning work in 1803. By 1810 his name was sketched across the shop's facia. The second half of the 19th century marked the gradual development of the wine business and the equally gradual disappearance of the

grocery trade. The last remaining stocks of groceries were sold to Fry's of Duke Street in 1896. At the beginning of the 20th century Francis Berry took full advantage of the opportunities presented overseas, including the U.S.A., where the firm's Cutty Sark blended Scotch whisky has since become a leading brand (see page 127).

Following the Great War Hugh Rudd joined the firm as a junior partner, bringing with him an expert knowledge of German wines. The firm, who hold a Royal Warrant, has had a long association with the Royal Household and was chosen in 1923 to furnish the wine cellar in Queen Mary's Doll's House, now at Windsor Castle. Everything was made exactly to scale, each bottle containing exactly what the bottle said it did.

A little must be said about Berry Bros. and Rudd's beautiful shop: the wood-panelled ground floor with its famous weighing beams and the shelf of books registering the weights of the famous from Byron to Lawrence Olivier; as well as the plaque in the passage from St. James's Street to Pickering Place, commemorating the

Big 'T'

Age: 12 years old.
Address: The Tomatin Distillery Company Ltd., Tomatin, Inverness-shire.
Available in the U.K. mostly in restaurants and hotels; in Europe, the U.S.A. and Japan.

For details, see 'Single malts'.

Delicate, mellow. Dark colour. Recommended without water as an after-dinner drink.

Blue Hanger

Address: Berry Bros. and Rudd Ltd., 3 St James's Street, London S.W.1.
Berry Bros. of London, and Houndmills, Basingstoke, supply Blue Hanger in the U.K.

This whisky is named after William Hanger, an 18th century dandy. He was called 'Blue' Hanger because the elegant clothes he wore were always in a variety of shades of blue. He was adjudged the best dressed man of his age and along with others of the Beau Monde, was a customer of Berry's.

Malty, smooth, clean taste, mellow, lingering taste. Medium colour. Recommended as an after-dinner drink or when cold or wet.

use of the upstairs by the Legation of the Government of Texas from 1842 to 1845 when it was accredited to the Court of King James; and the finely proportioned dining room on the first floor with its Cuban mahogony ceiling.

Mellow, refreshing, clean taste, smooth, malty.

death in 1908, his son Robert continued to build up the business.

Family involvement ended tragically when Robert was killed during the First World War. The company attracted the interest of the famous wine and spirit merchants W. and A. Gilbey Ltd. who eventually persuaded the last shareholder to sell, to become the owners by the end of the Second World War.

Mellow, full-bodied, smooth.

Chivas Regal

Age: 12 years old.
Address: Chivas Brothers, 111/113 Renfrew Road, Paisley.
Parent Company: The Seagram Company Ltd.
Available widely in the U.K. and abroad.

The man behind this successful brand was Samuel Bronfman who

The Buchanan Blend

Age: 8 years old.
Address: James Buchanan and Co. Ltd., Buchanan House, 3 St. James's Square, London S.W.1.
Parent company: Guinness plc.

For the story of James Buchanan, please see the history section of this book.

Tangy.

Catto's 12 Year Old

Age: 12 years old.
Address: James Catto and Co. Ltd., Renfrew.
Parent Company: International Distillers and Vintners Ltd.
Available in U.K. public houses, restaurants and from spirit retailers; exported widely, including to the U.S.A., Canada, France, Spain and Japan.

James Catto set up in business in Aberdeen more than 100 years ago, selling in Scotland and exporting to Scots overseas. He had friends in the shipping world and Catto's became a leading brand with the shipping companies – most notably P. and O. In 1900 the firm became a private limited company and after James's

created the Seagram empire. Strath-isla malt whisky is at the heart of Chivas Regal.

Slight sweetness, woody.

Cutty 12

Age: 12 years old.
Address: Berry Bros. and Rudd Ltd., 3 St. James's Street, London S.W.1.
Available in the U.K. direct from Berry Bros. in London, Houndmills and Basingstoke. It has 55 export markets worldwide.

For details, see 'Standard blends'.

Delicate, refreshing, light-bodied, clean taste, smooth. Pale colour.

Desmond and Duff De Luxe

Age: 12 years old.
Address: Clydesdale Scotch Whisky Co. Ltd., 8 Dorset Square, London N.W.1
Exported worldwide, including the U.S.A., France, Germany, Belgium, Japan and South America.

In the last 12 years Desmond and Duff De Luxe has received 12 gold medals in international competitions.

Mellow, full-bodied, clean taste, smooth, malty. Pale in colour. Recommended with a splash of water.

Dimple

Age: 12 years old.
Address: John Haig and Company Ltd., Haig House, Albany Street, Edinburgh.
Parent Company: Guinness plc.
This famous brand is known as **Pinch** in some markets.

Soft, lingering taste. Pale colour.

Findlater's 8 Year Old

Age: 8 years old.
Address: Findlater Mackie Todd and Co. Ltd., Windsor Avenue, Merton Abbey, London S.W.19.
Limited U.K. sales. Exported worldwide, especially to Spain, Japan and South America.

Unusually young for what the producers consider a de luxe blend. For more details, see 'Standard blends'.

Mellow.

Findlater's 12 Year Old

Age: 12 years old.

Address: Findlater Mackie Todd and Co. Ltd., Windsor Avenue, Merton Abbey, London S.W.19.

For details, see 'Standard blends'. Limited sales in the U.K., but exported worldwide.

Mellow.

Strathcona, John Grant, William's first-born son, went to Canada and succeeded in setting up contracts both in Canada and the U.S.A. In 1909 another export push was made when Charles Gordon spent a year in the yet largely unexplored export markets of the Far East and of Australia and New Zealand. In 1911 important agencies and selling facilities were negotiated in Europe. When war broke out in 1914 the company had established over sixty agencies in thirty different countries.

William Grant died in 1923 but his firm continued to prosper, overcoming the long years of prohibition (they would have nothing to do with bootleggers) by looking to the markets of the Far East. After World War II, when whisky was an important currency earner for the U.K., the family travelled worldwide increasing the popularity of Grant's blend still further. Today Grant's is sold in over 180 countries thanks to the early pioneering days.

Sweet, full-bodied, smooth, soft, pungent, well-balanced. Medium-dark in colour.

His Excellency 21 Years Old

Age: 21 years old.
Address: Bartels, Rawlings Export Ltd., 32-4 Borough High Street, London S.E.1.
Parent Company: Bartels Rawlings International.
Available in selected licensed premises and from spirit retailers in the U.K. Available in France, Germany, Spain, Singapore, South Africa and elsewhere.

Mellow, lingering taste, clean taste, smooth, malty. Reddish colour. Recommended without water as an after-dinner drink.

Islay Mist

Age: 8 years old.
Address: Long John Distilleries, Westhorn, 1780 London Road, Glasgow.
Parent Company: Whitbread and Co. plc.
Available in the U.K.

Grant's

Age: 12 years old (a version of Grant's Finest Scotch Whisky).
Address: William Grant and Sons Ltd., The Glenfiddich Distillery, Dufftown, Keith, Banffshire. Available in the U.K. in selected supermarkets and from spirit retailers. Abroad it is available duty-free and in most domestic markets throughout the world.

It was the spectacular crash of Pattison's in 1898, the biggest wholesale whisky merchants in the country and the biggest buyer of his whisky, which made up William Grant's mind expand the firm from distillers to wholesalers and blenders who supplied the retailers direct, and to explore the possibilities of exporting overseas. William Grant's second son Charles and his son-in-law Charles Gordon went south and with a lot of determination and shoe-leather sold the Grant's blend in Glasgow and Lancashire, where a Blackburn office was opened in 1904.

Armed with letters of introduction from his distant relative, the High Commissioner for Canada, Lord

Laphroaig (see 'Single malts') is said to be one of the constituents of this de luxe blend.

Smoky, peaty, full-bodied, aromatic, lingering taste, smooth. Dark colour.

John Begg Gold Cap

Age: 12 years old.
Address: John Begg Ltd., Trafalgar House, 75 Hope Street, Glasgow.
Parent company: Guinness plc. Available in the U.S.A., Belgium, Japan, Thailand and South Korea.

For details, see 'Single malts' and 'Standard blends'.

Delicate, mellow, clean taste, smooth. Dark in colour. Recommended with or without water, and with mixers.

Johnnie Walker Black Label

Age: 12 years old.
Address: John Walker and Sons Ltd., 63 St James's Street, London S.W.1.
Parent company: Guinness plc. Available in all types of U.K. outlets and exported worldwide.

Johnnie Walker Black Label is the world's best-selling de luxe whisky. It is a blend of 12 years old Scotch whisky and Cardhu Highland malt.

Mellow, smooth, malty. Dark in colour. Recommended with or without water or with ice.

Langs Select

Age: 12 years old.
Address: Lang Brothers Ltd., 100 West Nile Street, Glasgow.
Parent company: Robertson and Baxter Ltd.
Available from U.K. spirit retailers and on licensed premises; widely exported. Recently appointed Scotch whisky distillers to the Queen Mother.

Sherried, sweet, mellow, smooth, medium-bodied. Dark colour.

Logan

Address: White Horse Distillers Ltd., 99 Borron Street, Port Dundas, Glasgow.
Parent company: Guinness plc. Available in all types of U.K. outlets. Its export markets are Europe, U.S.A., Japan, Australia, Africa and South America.

This de luxe blend is made from about fifty different whiskies including Highland malts and lighter grains from the Lowlands.

Mellow, full-bodied, aromatic. Dark colour.

Mackinlay's Legacy

Age: 12 years old.
Address: Charles Mackinlay and Co. Ltd., 9/21 Salamander Place, Leith, Edinburgh.
Parent company: The Invergordon Distillers (Holdings) Ltd.
Available in the U.K. Exported worldwide.
For details, see 'Standard blends'.

Mellow, full-bodied, lingering taste, smooth, malty. Dark colour.
Recommended anytime but particularly satisfying after dinner.

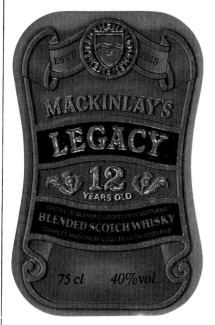

Milord's

Age: 12 years old.
Address: Macdonald and Muir Ltd., 186 Commercial Street, Leith, Edinburgh.
Parent company: Macdonald Martin Distilleries plc.
Exported to South America and elsewhere.

Milord's is one of the oldest names held by Macdonald and Muir Ltd. Its

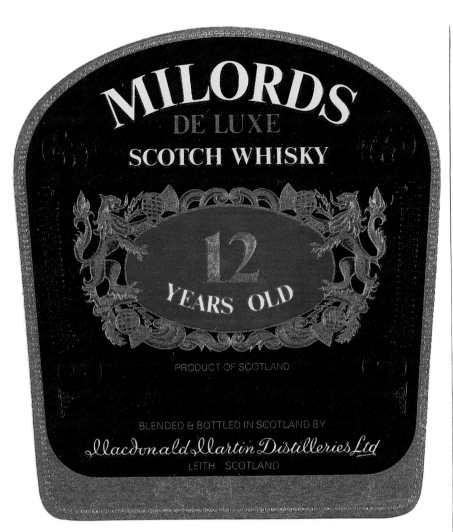

Ne Plus Ultra

Age: 12 years old.
Address: John Dewar and Sons
Ltd., Inveralmond, Perth.
Parent company: Guinness plc.
Sold primarily in Canada and Japan.

Ne Plus Ultra means, roughly trans-
lated, 'nothing more beyond' which
is intended to imply that it is the best.
The brand has been around for dec-
ades and is blended and bottled at the
company's Inveralmond plant, Perth.

Mellow, smooth.

origins date back to a prestigious
connection with the House of Lords
bar.

Mellow, smooth, medium-bodied.
Reddish colour.

Morton's Royal Mile

Age: 12 years old.
Address: George Morton Ltd.,
Chapel Bond, Eastern Road,
Montrose.
Parent company: Amalgamated
Distilled Products plc.
Available in the U.K. mainly on
licensed premises; exported to
Spain.

This product has been in the company's portfolio for over 50 years.
The malts used in the blend are
mainly from the Speyside area. The
name derives from Edinburgh's historic royal route.

Full-bodied, malty. Dark colour.

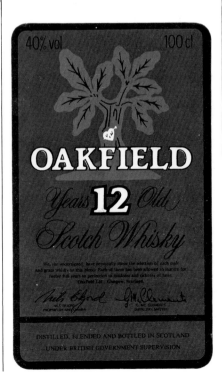

Oakfield 12 Years Old

Age: 12 years old.
Address: Oakfield Ltd., 100
Wellington Street, Glasgow.
Available in Scandinavia.

For more details, see 'Standard
blends'.

Delicate, mellow, light-bodied,
smooth. Pale colour. Recommended
with or without water.

Old Parr 500

Age: 15 years old.
Address: Macdonald Greenlees Ltd., 3a Palmerston Place, Edinburgh.
Parent company: Guinness plc. Export markets are the U.S.A., Europe, Asia and South America.

This brand is named after Thomas Parr who is buried in Westminster and is reputed to have lived for 152 years, dying in 1635.

Old Rarity De Luxe

Age: 12 years old.
Address: Bulloch Lade and Co. Ltd., Trafalgar House, 75 Hope Street, Glasgow.
Parent company: Guinness plc. Available from U.K. spirit retailers and on licensed premises; in the U.S.A., France, Italy, Trinidad and Venezuela.

Produced by an old, established blending company who proclaim: 'If a better Scotch exists, it is a well kept secret.' This brand is available in bottles and handsome stoneware jars. Caol Ila (see 'Single malts') is an essential ingredient of this well-respected de luxe blend.

Delicate, mellow, clean taste, smooth. Dark in colour. Recommended with or without water, and with mixers.

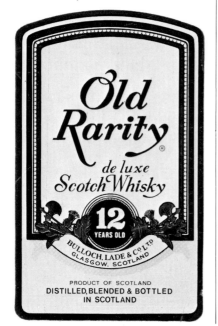

Old St. Andrews

Age: 12 years old.
Address: 144 Kirkdale, London S.E.26.
Available in selected U.K. wine stores; in the U.S.A., Europe, Canada, Japan, Australia, New Zealand and elsewhere.

The name Old St. Andrews is synonymous with golf and this brand has a distinctly golfing connection – packaging includes a hand-made leather golf bag and caddie cart and golf-ball miniatures in a six shot pack! There is also a one-litre bottle designed for air travel safety.

Full-bodied, lingering taste, clean taste, smooth. Reddish colour.

Pipe Major

Age: 12 years old.
Address: Montrose Whisky Company Ltd., 16B West Central Street, London W.C.1.
Exported worldwide.

Sweet, full-bodied, fruity. Dark colour. Recommended without water.

Putachieside

Age: 12 years old.
Address: William Cadenhead Ltd., 32 Union Street, Campbeltown, Argyll.
Available in speciality shops in the U.K. Abroad it is available mainly in the U.S.A., Germany and Holland.

Cadenhead's blend of whiskies known as Putachieside goes back over one hundred years. Unlike many brands which dropped it from their labels, Putachieside still retains the 'liqueur' tag.

Putachieside – the place – was to be found in Aberdeen and was later known as Carnegie's Brae. It was partly destroyed by the making of Union Street, the city's impressive main street, and finally cleared away by the construction of New Market Street in the 1840s. It has a delightful label which shows the Wallace Tower or Well House Tower, Netherkirkgate and Carnegie's Brae as they were in Victorian Aberdeen.

Delicate, lingering taste, smooth, full-bodied in the aftertaste. No colouring added.

Queen Elizabeth

Address: Avery's of Bristol Ltd., 7 Park Street, Bristol.
Available from U.K. spirit retailers and exported to Japan.

This company was established in 1793. Its Queen Elizabeth brand has been going for over 30 years but was, in fact, named after Queen Elizabeth I. The company began exporting to Japan in the 1980s, and claims to produce the first 100 per cent Scotch whisky in a 100 per cent Japanese package which includes a distinctive silkscreen printed bottle.

Delicate, peaty, mellow, smooth, malty. Straw gold colour. Recommended with water.

Rob Roy

Address: Stanley P. Morrison, Springburn Bond, Carlisle Street, Glasgow.
Available in Scotland at present, but there are plans to broaden its markets.

Rob Roy contains the three single malts from Morrison's Bowmore, Auchentoshan and Glengarioch distilleries. One to watch for.

Smooth, mellow.

Royal Bond

Age: over 8 years old.
Address: Clydesdale Scotch Whisky Co. Ltd., 8 Dorset Square, London N.W.1.
Worldwide export markets, including Europe and the U.S.A.

Mellow, full-bodied, clean taste, smooth, malty. Pale in colour.

Royal Choice

Age: 21 years old.
Address: Long John Distilleries, Westthorn, 1780 London Road, Glasgow.

Parent company: Whitbread and Co. plc.
Available in international and domestic duty-free outlets; exported to France and the Far East and duty-free outlets in U.S.A., Europe and the U.K.

Launched in 1982 primarily as a duty-free and export brand. It is presented in a specially commissioned Spode Royal Blue decanter bottle finished in 22 carat gold and packaged in a blue suede box with gold silk lining!

Mellow, smooth.

St. James's

Age: 12 years old.
Address: Berry Bros. and Rudd Ltd., 3 St. James's Street, London S.W.1.
Available in the U.K. from Berry Bros. and Rudd Ltd., 3 St. James's Street, London, and Houndmills, Basingstoke; exported to the Far East and South America.

St. James's comes in a replica of an 18th century hand-blown bottle from the company collection of historic bottles. The bottle label shows St. James's Palace which is in the vicinity of Berry Bros. who have had a long association with royalty and are Royal Warrant holders. St. James's is also packed in an elegant carton showing

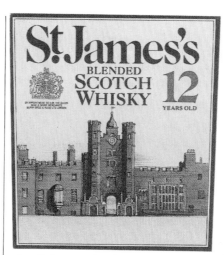

the Palace and other typical scenes from the St. James's area.

Peaty, clean taste, smooth, dry, medium-bottled.

Something Special

Age: 12 years old.
Address: Hill, Thomson and Co. Ltd., 45 Frederick Street, Edinburgh.
Parent company: The Seagram Company Ltd.
Limited sales in the U.K. – mainly specialist outlets, selected hotels and bars; exported worldwide.
For details, see 'Standard blends'.

Mellow, clean taste, smooth, malty, medium-bottled. Amber colour.

Spey Cast

Age: 12 years old.
Address: Gordon and MacPhail, 58-60 South Street, Elgin.
Available from U.K. spirit retailers and other specialist outlets; various export markets – mainly European.

An award-winning blend from the G. and M. stable. As well as bottles, an Admirals' Brass Two-bottle Mahogany Tantalus containing a decanter of Spey Cast and another of 1956 Smith's Glenlivet, is also available.

Refreshing, clean taste, quite malty. Recommended as a pre-dinner drink.

Swing

Address: John Walker and Sons Ltd., 63 St. James's Street, London S.W.1.
Parent company: Guinness plc.
Available in specialist outlets in the U.K. and exported worldwide.

Swing is known as **Celebrity** in some countries. The convex base of the distinctive Swing bottle means that it will swing gently when touched. It was specially produced to suit the transatlantic liners of the 1920s; the bottle would remain upright regardless of the temperament of the sea.

Smoky, mellow, smooth. Reddish colour. Recommended with or without water or with ice.

Usher's

Age: 12 years old.

Address: J. and G. Stewart, 21 Manor Place, Edinburgh.
Parent company: Guinness plc.
Mainly intended for export.

For details see 'Standard blends'.

Usquaebach

Address: Douglas Laing and Co. Ltd., 35 Robertson Street, Glasgow.
Parent company: Twelve Stone Flagons Ltd.
Available in the U.K. at Heathrow Airport; widely exported, including, conspicuously, to the People's Republic of China. It can be bought in crystal decanters and flagons.

The proprietor of Usquaebach, Stanley J. Stankiwicz, was an unemployed plywood salesman from Pittsburgh when in 1969 he read that Usquaebach had been served at President Nixons' Inauguration. Scotch was Stanley's hobby – he claims to have the largest single collection of single malt Scotch whiskies in the

world! By 1973 he had managed to buy the Usquaebach trademark and blend formula. At first no American

distributor would touch the drink. But in 1974 he offered Prince Rainier of Monaco a case to celebrate an important anniversary, was granted an audience and won over Elizabeth Taylor who was also present, to the merits of the drink. She introduced it to the late Rock Hudson who apparently loved it! The rest, as they say, is history . . . The brand name is intriguing, the word 'Usquaebach' being derived from the original Gaelic for 'whisky'.

Delicate, sweet, mellow, lingering taste, clean taste, smooth. Medium dark in colour. Recommended without water, possibly as an after-dinner drink.

Vat 69 Reserve

Age: 12 years old.
Address: Wm. Sanderson and Son Ltd., South Queensferry, West Lothian.
Parent company: Guinness plc.

The story of Vat 69 can be found in the history section of this book (see page 19).

Dry, medium-bodied.

White Heather

Address: White Heather Distilleries Ltd., The House of Campbell, West Byrehill, Kilwinning, Ayrshire.
Parent company: Pernod-Ricard.
Widely available in the U.K. Exported throughout Europe, especially to France.

Well-balanced.

Whyte and Mackay De Luxe

Address: Whyte and Mackay Distillers, Dalmore House, 296-8 St. Vincent Street, Glasgow.
Parent company: Lonrho plc.
Available in all U.K. outlets and abroad, including duty-free shops.

For details, see 'Standard blends'.

Sherried, mellow, full-bodied, lingering taste, smooth. Dark colour.

INDEX